TAKE ANOTHER LOOK

A SCRIPTURAL REVIEW OF TRADITIONAL CHRISTIAN DOCTRINE

David Hulse, D.D.

AuthorHouse™
1663 Liberty Drive
Bloomington, IN 47403
www.authorhouse.com
Phone: 1-800-839-8640

© 2010 David Hulse, D.D.. All rights reserved.

No part of this book may be reproduced, stored in a retrieval system, or transmitted by any means without the written permission of the author.

First published by AuthorHouse 4/19/2010

ISBN: 978-1-4520-0705-2 (e)
ISBN: 978-1-4520-0704-5 (sc)
ISBN: 978-1-4520-0703-8 (hc)

Library of Congress Control Number: 2010904372

Printed in the United States of America
Bloomington, Indiana

This book is printed on acid-free paper.

Light Within Ministries
3195 Dayton Xenia Rd Ste 900-331
Dayton OH 45434
937-912-9229

www.lightwithin.com

A companion study guide is available FREE at www.lightwithin.com/look_book.htm

This guide can also be used for small study groups.

Contents

Acknowledgments	ix
Preface	xi

TAKE ANOTHER LOOK   1

A Scriptural Review of Law and Grace	1
God -- Master of Heart or Law?	3
Law vs. Grace	6

THE RESURRECTION   15

The First Resurrection	19
The Spiritual and Natural Worlds Coming Together	26

WHAT DOES HINDER THEE?   29

Reality vs. Unreality	29
The Realm of Appearance	31
Awakening From the Dream	37
The City is Your Own	41
Beyond Thinking	47

HELL YES? HELL NO?   53

History of the Fundamental Doctrine of Hell	53
What is God's Judgment?	55
A Place of Correction	59

The Lake of Fire	61
Deliverance from Hell	64
Appearance of the Anti-Christ	66
The Many Bodies of Christ	68

AGREE WITH YOUR ADVERSARY — 71

How to Stay Out of Prison	77
Love Thy Enemy	81

RELEASING SPIRITS — 83

Reconciliation	85
Releasing Spirits	88
The Other Side Of The Coin	96

THE POINT OF RETURN — 99

The Great Returning	99
Cleansing Of The High Place	115
From Knowledge To Expression	131
Back Into The Upper Room	140
Conclusion	144
LWM Message-of-the-Month	147
About The Author… David Hulse, D.D.	149

Dedication

This book is dedicated to my mother, Bea, who has been a great support throughout my 40+ years of ministry. Because of her love and friendship, I have been able to follow a path of searching for Truth.

Thank you, Mother. I love you and appreciate your dedication. You made it possible for me to be where I am today.

Acknowledgments

Taking this book, which started in the form of several booklets, and turning it into one book, has truly been an experience in community. My grateful thanks and appreciation to so many for the many hours spent in the preparation of this book.

My thanks to Brenda Dupuy – Peterson (Jacks), for editing and transcribing the original booklets.

The following "light workers" assisted in editing, proof-reading, and/or feedback: Kristina Arntz, Karen Atkinson, Mark Eaton, Kelli Jack, Hjordis Jansson, Linda Norton & Donna Peterson. My appreciation to all.

My appreciation also goes to Tim Leach for making all the changes in the computer and for preparing the book for printing.

Thank you Hannah Simmons who donated to have this book published professionally.

My grateful appreciation to each of the above for being part of this project!

Sincerely,

David

Preface

I realize that this book may not be for everyone at this time. However, it is necessary to challenge the sensibilities of man-made traditions, which have made the word of present truth of no effect to this generation.

I ask that you listen to your own inner Christ intelligence which is able to lead you into all truth, rather than listening to the feeble attempts of men's voices on the paths that seem right, who are only plunging us into the depths of unanswered questions, ever learning, but never able to come to the knowledge of the truth.

In this day, there are several versions of the Bible. I suggest choosing the version which best suits your understanding of language. II Timothy 2:15 says: Study to shew thyself approved unto God, a workman that needeth not to be ashamed, rightly dividing the word of truth. The study presented in this book is based on the "Thompson Chain-Reference Bible", "Strong's Exhaustive Concordance of the Bible", the guidance of the inner teacher – the Holy Spirit, and spiritual *common sense*. The result has challenged much of the second-handed information that has been passed down through Christian patriarchy. This scripture also mentions, "rightly dividing the word of truth". To do this, we need to discern which scriptures are inspired by God and which scriptures contain man's perceptions and hidden political and cultural agenda's.

> All scripture *is* given by inspiration of God, and *is* profitable for doctrine, for reproof, for correction, for instruction in righteousness. (II Timothy 3:16 KJV)

The Greek lexicon shows us that translators omitted a comma after the word scripture and added the word *is* in the King James Version. Therefore, the scripture should read, in its proper context, "All scripture, given by inspiration of God and profitable for doctrine…." It is important to note that italicized words indicate that the translators or KJV have added them.

Western religious thought has put a great emphasis on the masculinity of God. For the sake of language and the flow of reading, the pages that follow mostly address God in the masculine form. However, I honor and acknowledge the Goddess/Mother aspect of deity, (as shown in the name – El Shaddai, (the large and many-breasted one) that I equally celebrate in spirit.

If you are in the process of re-examining old childhood beliefs and have realized there has to be a "more excellent way", this book is for you. With this in mind, I invite you to "Take Another Look" at some of the most important tenants of fundamental Judeo-Christian dogma. We will explore these basic ideas from the cultural context in which they were experienced and written, as well as the influences of the translators. This will take us from a fear-based message to the Gospel, or good news, of a love-based premise.

Author

> Who also hath made us able ministers of the New Testament; not of the letter, but of the spirit: for the letter killeth, but the spirit giveth life.
> [2Corinthians 3:6]

TAKE ANOTHER LOOK

A Scriptural Review of Law and Grace

We will never move on to understand our perfection (wholeness) until we establish ourselves in the principles of the true teachings of the universal Christ. We have invested a great deal of time laying our foundation on the shifting sands of second-handed, passed-down information, rather than on the solid rock of our ability to show ourselves approved. Due to a perception of a separate God, we have focused on what we can get from God, rather than on what we can give to God. We have not considered His heart and His desires. We have forgotten that relationship is a two-way street where God is concerned.

> "Not unto us, O Lord, not unto us, but unto your name give glory..." Psalms 115:1

Present truth is experienced when the inherent Word enters our consciousness from Spirit, tuning the soul (mind) to the same vibration of Spirit, making them one. From this union, the body follows. The word that brings this revelation is not just another revelation about God, but is a word that reveals the heart of God. The heart of God is saying, "I thirst and hunger for a people to be my body. I desire an availability to express my love, mercy and grace to humanity at an earth level."

God's desire is to speak to us face to face. Yet, we have used the law and letter of the word in such a way that we have drifted away from God. He does not need the word to be condensed or watered down by religious interpretations. The law is not the heart of God. The spoken and written words of the law were intended to bring humanity to know its need for God. The realm of prophecy, gifts, miracles and healing is seeing where God has been, but it is not *seeing* God in the present. Let's go a step further. The so-called five-fold ministry has been given for perfection, but we, as a spiritual creation, are already perfect as our Creator is perfect! Certainly, there is a need for ministry and gatherings, but their purpose is only to remind each of us how to know God in ourselves.

We have settled for "a" blessing long enough. "A" blessing includes the temporal gifts such as prophecy and physical healing. "THE" blessing is eternal and life evermore. (Ps. 133) The fact that we are born into this earth gives us the God-given right to life. You do not have to earn immortality; *it is your identity*. A ministry which teaches that healing and deliverance can only come through the ministry of another man, short-changes its people. God is ready to reveal Himself in His sons to deliver creation from the limitations imposed by the law. God's will is for life and immortality to be brought to manifestation! He is ready to reveal the Word in its purest essence. We will begin to experience true manifestation as people tune into their oneness with God.

> "Come now and let us reason together saith the Lord. Though your sins be as scarlet, they shall be white as snow, though they be red like crimson, they shall be as wool. If ye be willing and obedient ye shall eat the good of the land." Isaiah 1:18-19

This scripture does not refer to people just getting together to reason out their problems. But rather, it is a call from God to man to communicate His heart. All that is required from us is our willingness to leave our doctrines of law and legalism as interpreted by human perception. Are you willing to meet God at the reasoning table of the heart? God doesn't want His Word being twisted and used to build great organizations that use "thus saith God" to hold people captive to its hidden agendas. God is ready to direct your thinking toward ways that will resonate deep inner truths. It is time to drop our pretenses and stop being religious with God. It is time to communicate with God face to face.

God -- Master of Heart or Law?

"And the Lord said unto Moses, Go unto the people and sanctify them... and be ready... for the third day the Lord will come down in the sight of all the people upon Mt. Sinai." Exodus 19:10-11

"And all the people saw the thunderings, and the lightenings and the noise of the trumpet and the mountain smoking. When the people saw it, they removed and stood afar off. And they said unto Moses, speak thou with us and we will hear, but let God not speak with us, lest we die... And the people stood afar off and Moses drew near unto the thick darkness where God was." Exodus 20:18

God desired to speak with Israel face to face, but they were not able to deal directly with the *voice* of God. They were afraid, so they rejected God on a first-hand basis. Instead, they wanted Moses to go to the mountain, come down, and tell them what God had said. This is when the *pollution* of the Word of God began.

However, we must take into consideration that the Bible is only an interpretation of whatever God would have actually said. Our scriptures do not contain the words *written with the finger of God*. Today, preachers speak of law and legalism as they carve their own interpretations of God's law into the minds of their followers by adding "thus saith the Lord". In truth, what they share about the laws of God is their human interpretation of the law, which is based on another's human interpretation. It is this cycle that leads us away from the heart (intent) of God.

Let us consider a serious question. If the word of God, with all of the law and legalism of religion, would have been able to bring the whole world to God, why haven't more people responded? Untold thousands have left the church, feeling hopeless from not being able to bow to this God of law and legalism. Religion, standing in its self-righteousness, has turned many people away from, rather than to God.

God gave the law to Moses to improve the condition of human kind. It was *not* given to institute a way to God, or to confine society into religious sects. It was given that we might see ourselves and understand our need for a relationship with God.[1]

The law says, "thou shall not steal". Consider the situations of two people, one who is responsible and one who is not. The responsible man wants to work but, for some reason beyond his control, he is not able to. His family is hungry and, out of desperation, he takes fruit from a food stand. He is caught, arrested and brought before the law. The irresponsible man is lazy and feels the world owes him a living. He takes fruit from the same stand and is also caught, arrested and brought before the law. Is it fair that the law applies equally to both persons? Grace would look at each situation individually. There is record in the history of the scriptures, that God allowed a lying spirit to come upon man, and other times, lying was not permissible by law.[2] What about David? David is considered to have been a man after God's own heart. Yet he committed adultery, murdered and ate the forbidden shewbread of the temple. According to the law, all of these actions were punishable by death. Why was David not put to death? Because he was king? No! David was a man who knew and followed the heart of the Most High. He did not live by the law and was therefore not judged nor punished by this law. However, he did pay for his mistakes through the life of his own son. He reaped what he had sown, just as we all do. The key here is that there is a difference in reaping what you sow, and being judged by God. Nobody gets by. To every action there is a reaction. It is time to grow up and take responsibility for what we sow.

---

1   Please read Galatians 3:23-26
2   *II Chronicles 18:22, Joshua 2:4*

We need to see behind the letter of the law and into the heart of God. We can never be righteous by our works; righteousness is only found by allowing the God within to manifest.

> "Sacrifice and offerings thou didst not desire, mine ears thou hast opened, burnt offerings and sin offerings thou hast not required." Psalms 40:6

> "Sacrifice and offerings thou wouldest not, but a body thou hast prepared. In burnt offerings and sacrifices for sin, thou hast no pleasure… He taketh away the first, that He might establish the second." Hebrews 10:5-9

The Old Testament law speaks of sacrifice and sin offerings repeatedly. But God said that was never MY heart! Again, these things were only given that humankind might see the hopelessness in reaching God by their own works. When Jesus fulfilled the law, it was in a different cultural time period. Religion no longer preaches the need to sacrifice animals, but it does preach the need for your entire life to be one of sacrifice and walking the "crucified way". This is just another way of making sin offerings in an effort to appease God and make humankind worthy. Even under the old covenant, God became weary of the human effort and declared, "I never desired these things."

If we choose to live in law consciousness, we need to keep the whole law. In law consciousness, if you break one law, you are guilty of all.[3] The reason we see so many Christians miserable is because they confess a belief for the law and yet cannot live by it. By their own terms, they walk in condemnation. With the law, religion has pointed a finger to those who need help with not breaking the law. It is a fact that some people are habitual liars and others are kleptomaniacs, etc. But, according to the law of religion, we condemn even those people whom we know are in a prison of their own. The heart of God wants us to *stop judging* and *start loving*.

There is a Universal Law of reaping and sowing that has absolutely nothing to do with religion, free will, belief or disbelief. It is a law of nature that a seed sown will produce fruit of the same kind. This

---

3   James 2:10

Universal Law is not God sending punishment to us; it is *our own experience* of correction. (Jer. 2:19) There is no annihilation and eternal punishment set from the wrath of God for us to endure! We endure the consequences of our own actions, and we learn from these experiences.

Jesus was in the wilderness for forty days and nights just before His time of manifestation. It was here where He was tempted. The wilderness was that part of His mind where the temptation rose to use His power to prove He was the Son of God. Now remember, Jesus was raised during a time when the law was the prevalent mind-set of the culture. This belief system, which originated outside of himself, became adversarial to the experience of what was being fathered within. As He began His move toward the ending of the law, He brought in the testament of grace.

Law vs. Grace

> "The anointing which ye have received of Him abideth in you and **ye need not that any man teach you**, but as the same anointing teacheth you all things and is truth and is no lie and even as it hath taught you, ye shall abide in Him." I John 2:27

> "This is He that came by water and blood, even Jesus Christ...and it is the Spirit that beareth witness, because **the Spirit is truth**." I John 5:6

As we awaken in the midst of religious doctrines, it is important to realize that we are *returning* to the house of God. To return somewhere, we had to have been there before. As the purity of the word of God reveals itself, it is not any man who teaches us this word, but the *anointing within* that brings all of these things to our remembrance. God has called forth a ministry of instructors and through the witness of spirit, has enabled us to awake from the stupor of religious doctrine. This quest for truth will always be in opposition to religious programming. Our security lies in the fact that no matter how much our religious mind may disagree, the anointing abides deep within and is the Spirit of truth that always bears witness.

Look at what the scriptures say concerning law and grace. Many of these scriptures do not need comment; they speak for themselves if we simply look at what they say rather than listening to the parroting of religious theories and ideas.

> "You who are trying to be justified by the law, have been alienated from Christ. You have fallen from grace."
> Galatians 5:4

We have all sat in pews and taken in the sermons about our fall from grace. But according to the scripture, as long as we depend upon our works to make us acceptable to God, we *alienate* ourselves from the grace of Christ.

> "Are you so foolish, after beginning with the spirit, are you now trying to attain your goal by human effort?"
> Galatians 3:3 (Amplified)

Do not forget that first and foremost, you are spirit! Your efforts in the human form are only those of the spirit experiencing humanity. What is true and whole about you has never changed, and never will. Remember your spirit and you remember who you truly are. When we remember who it is we are, then we naturally respond to one another in a state of grace. We do not need to rely on the conditions of the law to feel acceptable to God, we know that we are acceptable because we are a part of the whole that *is* God!

Many people who have accepted the plan of salvation still attempt to *reclaim* their salvation whenever they feel that have had a bad thought or behaved in a way that is not in accordance with the law. We need to set aside our belief in repentance and move on to perfection[4] (wholeness)

---

4 *Hebrews 6:1-2*

which already exists. Religion can hold people in a state of mind that they go to bed not knowing if they are "saved" or "lost". How many times have you left a meeting where such condemnation was preached that you walked away wondering if you had ever really had an experience with God or had received valid salvation? Condemnation comes through looking to human efforts to make you "good enough" to please God. The law will always make you feel ungodly, pointing out your faults, frailties and human weaknesses. The law takes your eyes off from grace and directs them to your works! This is the greatest weakness of the Christian world.

There is a so-called "gift" working in the church. Some call it "the gift of discernment" (spirit) but, in reality, it is the gift of suspicion (psychic). When God gives true discernment concerning a person or situation, it is given with compassion and love-- *never* with judgment. Discernment is the ability to look past appearance and see the Christ in another. This brings healing to the mind of the observer, who is then released of all condemnation.

> "And there came a voice to him, Rise, Peter, kill and eat. Peter said not so lord, for I have never eaten anything that is common or unclean. And the voice spake unto him again the second time, what God hath cleansed, that call not thou common. This was done thrice."
> Acts 10:13-16

In the eyes of God, all of humankind is clean, holy and righteous because God is all of these things. God sees us in our finished state of creation. When Peter saw a vision of the unclean beasts and was told to kill and eat them, he answered, "But Lord, I can't eat the unclean. I have a good reputation. I have kept the law and I am not about to break it now." God answered Peter, "I said arise and eat. Get up out of that place of law, legalism and externalism and arise!" Arise means to raise our own consciousness within. We rise from a legalistic religious mind into a spiritual, heavenly mind to see the world through God's eyes; the eyes of love and grace.

The scriptures say that you will know a man by his fruit-- not by his self-righteous works. What is the fruit? Love, joy, peace, longsuffering, kindness, goodness, faith, meekness, temperance-- against such, there is no law! A person who finds that life comes by the grace of God and taps into the nature of God will manifest these fruits. There is no law necessary to produce good works through them because the nature of God produces after its own kind.

> "We know that the law is good if a man uses it properly. We also know that the law is not for good men, but for law breakers, rebels, the ungodly and sinners." I Timothy 1:8

> "...the law worketh wrath, where there is no law, there is no transgression." Romans 4:15

> "...the strength of sin is the law." I Corinthians 15:56

> "For sin shall have no dominion over you, for you are not under the law but under grace." Romans 6:14

Take a serious look at what the scriptures have to say concerning sin, law, and grace. Religion uses the law to keep the good people "in line". Yet we read that the law was not given for the good or the righteous man. *The only strength that sin has is the law.* Take away the law, and you literally take away the power to sin, for where there is no law, there is no transgression! Sin has no dominion over the person who moves from the law into grace.

> "Through the law, we become conscious of sin." Romans 3:20

The only reason that we see sin everywhere is because we live in the law consciousness. Whatever consciousness we live in is what we manifest in life. Religion has made its mark on the world; we see every action through the perception of the law. We see evil everywhere and feel inclined to strike back at everything and everyone. The mind has been deceived to the point of believing that it is necessary to retaliate against the thought of something evil; evil becomes good through the distorted eyes of the religious mind. In other words, when we view something that we believe is evil to God, we believe that it is good to render evil back, thus rendering evil for evil. Evil only breeds more evil.

Proverbs tells us that a soft answer turns away wrath. Evil will never overcome evil. It takes good to overcome evil. Hate breeds more hate, resentment breeds more resentment and anger breeds more anger. Who will turn the tide? How long will you accept the persons of the wicked? (Ps. 82) How long will you see them as being evil, through the eyes of the law? When you see the "wicked" through the eyes of grace, you can no longer accept them as being wicked. Religion will surely fight you over this message. Why? Because this truth challenges all that evil has been built upon for thousands of years. When grace manifests and becomes reality, we are not captive to dead orders. Instead, the message of love, grace, mercy and reconciliation rules our life. Stop worrying about the actions of others and be true to the purpose God has placed in you to love unconditionally. It is time to leave the realm of eating from the tree of the knowledge of good and evil. It is knowledge that brings death-- not good and evil. Every time we gossip about someone or allow another person to gossip to us about someone else, we are eating of the knowledge that brings death. God is not concerned with the good or the evil, because it all must go. It is much easier for us to turn away from evil than good, but through the eyes of God, both good and evil are only the *fruit of the same tree.* Turn away from the tree of the knowledge of good and evil and eat from the tree of life.

You cannot become conscious of God through the law. Attempting to keep the law does not keep your mind on God; it keeps your mind on the actions of the flesh and holds you in the captivity of sin. It is time to focus on God and release our thoughts of law and sin. "The law made nothing perfect, but the bringing in of a better hope did, by which we draw nigh to God."[5] You cannot draw nigh to God through the eyes of law. Perfection does not come through law, but through *grace.*

> "Let us draw near with a true heart in full assurance of faith, having our hearts sprinkled from an evil conscious and our bodies washed with pure water." Hebrews 10:22

---

5   *Hebrews 7:19*

It is time for us to start believing that God fulfills promises. Hold to your faith without wavering. The only thing that can cause you to waver is to live in a consciousness of law and flesh. Know that God *is*. It does not matter what you see. Approach God with full assurance. Allow your consciousness to be cleansed, and as it is, your body will be washed with the pure water of God's word. Imagine the word of God undefiled by human religious interpretations! The very things that we have worked to "fix" would resolve themselves if we would allow our hearts to be cleansed from an evil law consciousness.

The only time we see Jesus show anger in the Bible was toward the religious money-changers in the temple. On the other hand, He embraced those whom the religious system rejected. Jesus didn't have any problem with the whoremongers, prostitutes, tax collectors and the "BIG" sinners. Why? First of all, because they were real and secondly, because the law helped them see where corrections needed to be made in order to bring them into spiritual alignment. It is religion that does not realize the law is alienating its people from the long awaited Messiah. Religious figures of all kinds have alienated themselves from the very One they preach about in their pulpit. They focus their message on law and external works. They do not really know God because their law has separated them from God. All that they know is what religion has handed down to them from one generation to the next. The heart of God is love, grace, mercy and reconciliation. Once the heart of God is revealed, the damage done by the misinterpretation of the word will be repaired and our true spiritual relationship will be restored.

> "The law came by Moses, but grace and truth came by Jesus Christ." John 1:17

How clear can it be? Moses gave the law; Jesus came and gave the *truth* about the law. The truth is grace. Moses gave us the *form* of righteousness. Jesus gave us the *substance* of righteousness. As long as we continue the attempt of attaining righteousness by law, we are rejecting the Christ self within us which is our righteousness. Feeling the need to "be good" in order to find favor with God uproots the whole foundation of grace. Grace is God's unmerited favor.

[handwritten note: no, grace is God's ability]

> "The thief cometh not, but for to steal, and to kill, and to destroy: I am come that ye might have life and that they might have it more abundantly." John 10:10

Jesus was not a lawgiver. He was a life giver. When religion wanted to stone, He gave life. Jesus, as a man, was raised under the teachings of the law, but his Christ nature could not help but offer pardon and forgiveness by grace and understanding. Through the eyes of grace, we do not see the manifestation of evil or sin; we look past the realm of fleshly appearances and see the reality of spirit, which is perfect and whole. Beholding through the eyes of grace, we become the life giver, we lay down law and we stop judging and condemning. The thief has killed and destroyed long enough. Become a life giver. Know that when enough people behold creation through the eyes of grace, we will see the human race come to the truth of grace.

Legalism is the idea that by human wisdom and effort, we can apply and live up to the standards of the "Christian life". It is the belief that through self-control and discipline we will become acceptable to God. Legalism is humanistic in that it asserts human power and sovereignty instead of the sovereignty of God. Christians tend to become discouraged and fall into sin because legalism is a joyless walk. It lacks the power of God and holds humanity in sin. It is the perversion of righteousness. It is modern Phariseeism. What is Jesus' answer to this?

> "Woe unto you scribes, Pharisees, hypocrites! For ye pay tithe of mint and anise and cumin, and have omitted the weightier matters of the law; judgment, mercy and faith… Woe unto you scribes, Pharisees, hypocrites! Ye make clean the outside of the cup, but within they are full of extortion and excess. Thou blind Pharisees cleanse first that which is within that the outside may be clean also… Even so outwardly ye appear righteous unto men, but within ye are full of hypocrisy and iniquity." Matthew 23:23-28

The religious mindset does not want a message of "freedom from law" ministered. It fears that humanity will use it as a license to sin, but this is not true. Holding humanity in the rules of law and legalism has caused us to depend upon human effort to attain righteousness. Clean the inside first and the outside will also be cleansed. Become concerned with mercy and faith in God's ability--not your ability-- and your whole life will be revolutionized.   ˡgrace

> "Moreover the law entered, that the offense might abound. But where sin did abound, grace did much more abound."
> Romans 5:20

> "The law was put in charge, to lead us to Christ, that we might be justified by faith." Galatians 3:24

The law was given to lead us to Christ by letting us know our need for Christ. When we discover that it is impossible to attain righteousness by the law, we can do either of two things: we can deny this and hide behind our own self righteousness, becoming locked into legalism; or, we can acknowledge our human frailties, turn to God and allow the righteousness of God to become our covering. God is the essence of our true nature: love. Humanity has had its way. It is God's time to reveal and manifest that which we already are, but have forgotten with all of our laws and legalism. The age of grace will be fulfilled and the age of righteousness will begin. Righteousness is a *right relationship* with God. Let it be settled in our minds that a right relationship with God cannot develop until we know the *heart* of God, accept grace, and turn from the bondage of law and legalism. As we do these things, grace will bring perfection to light, and we will step into the day of righteousness.

> "Owe no man anything but to love one another, for he that loveth another hath fulfilled the law...Love worketh no ill to His neighbor, therefore love is the fulfilling of the law." Romans 13:8,10

> "Hatred stirreth up strife, but love covereth all sins."
> Proverbs 10:12

> "Love… rejoiceth not in iniquity, but rejoiceth in truth… Love…beareth all things…" I Corinthians 13:6-7
>
> "And though I have the gift of prophecy and understand all mysteries and all knowledge, and though I have all faith so that I could move mountains and have not love, I am nothing." I Corinthians 13:2
>
> "And to know the love of Christ which passeth knowledge, that ye might be filled with all the fullness of God." Ephesians 3:19

Law has no love for humanity unless it appears to be living up to its standards. Law never covers sin. It rejoices in discovering adultery, and it takes pleasure in revealing sin. Grace loves humanity for it sees each through the eyes of God as perfect and whole. Grace knows no hatred and takes away all sin, for it sees no sin. Grace pardons and grants mercy, which brings the power to "go and sin no more".

Religion prides itself with gifts of prophecy and faith that can move mountains yet it knows nothing of the love of God, which can only be experienced through a revelation of the grace of God. It is not enough to understand all mysteries and to have all knowledge, which is only known through the grace of God. Without love, we have nothing. There is a realm, a dimension, a place of knowing the love of God by experience that surpasses all knowledge. It is in this place that we are filled with the fullness of God. The answer is not in how great our gifts are, how strong our faith is or how much knowledge we have; it is in finding and tuning in to the heart of God. The heart of God is in the people of humanity who walk in grace and love. When compassion fills our own lives, we find the heart of God. This is *grace*.

THE RESURRECTION

"What is man that thou art mindful of him?" (Ps. 8:4) Before we can understand the resurrection, we must understand who and what man is now. In the first chapter of Genesis we read, "Let us make man in our image, after our likeness." God is spirit. We are spirit. Revelations will take us nowhere until we understand this principle. The physical body is only the house in which you reside. In reality, it is spirit at a very low vibration.

Paul tells us in the fifth chapter of II Corinthians that if our earthly house (our body at a low vibration) is dissolved, we have a house made for us by God, eternal in the heavens, or in the realm of spirit at a higher vibration. Our true essence is eternal. Neither disease, nor destruction, nor death can bring an end to spirit. Our spiritual house, or spiritual body, is God residing within us. While we remain in our earthly house, we groan with its pain and limitations. We constantly desire to be clothed with our spiritual house. The cry of Paul's heart was to be clothed in his spiritual house, so as not to be found naked at the resurrection. (11 Cor. 5) As we are clothed with our spiritual house, which is simply allowing spirit to be in control, we can say, as did Paul, "Oh death, where is thy sting? Oh grave, where is thy victory?" (1Cor. 1:55) We must pass through the realm of thinking the physical body is the real person. We must understand our reality is our spiritual body.

Death has devastated many lives when a person loses contact with a loved one's physical body. In what we call death, the body returns to the dust from which it was taken and the spirit to God who gave it.[6] Death loses it sting when we come to the understanding that physical existence is neither the beginning nor the end of existence. What we call death is nothing more than the ending of a limited perception of space and time and the beginning of eternity. When the spirit enters the physical realm, it becomes limited by time and space. When it leaves this realm, it leaves time and limitation. The person who leaves the physical realm is just as alive as one in the physical body.[7] In fact, the person who has been "clothed upon" with a spiritual body is <u>more</u> alive than one who remains caught in the physical body with the limitations of time and space.

Since we are spirit, when we exit the physical body there is no need for us to return to the same body, as some religions have taught. Those we have known and loved, who have passed on to the other side, will not be resurrected into their old physical bodies. The physical body, in which we knew them as mother, father, sister or brother, returns to the dust, only leaving them with their spiritual body.[8] In the resurrection of Jesus, he took on many different forms. Once he was a gardener, another time he appeared as a traveler on the road to Emmaus. He appeared in many different forms.[9] Nevertheless, his friends did not recognize him in the form that he had taken until he spoke to them through his *spiritual* person-- they knew him by his spirit.

When we remember our departed loved ones, we hold the memories of their physical bodies in our minds. But we need to remember the true essence of our loved ones, not only their bodies. It is their *essence* that we will meet again. We must release our minds from the limitations of the physical experience. The realms of the spirit world are far greater than those of the physical world. When we release our thoughts from the focus of the physical realm, the boundaries of our physical form are removed; we *know* that the natural and spiritual worlds are *only separated by the mind's veil of unbelief.*

---

6 *Ecclesiastes 12:7*
7 *Matthew 22:32*
8 *I Corinthians 15:38*
9 *Mark 16:12*

You are spirit. To know yourself as spirit is the only true way to know God. And to know yourself, you must pass through the veil of flesh and go *within*. We miss reality when we only look after the needs of the physical body. Consider the hours of the day spent taking care of the needs of the body. We clothe it, feed it, keep it warm and even pamper it! How well we know ourselves in the flesh! But how well do we know ourselves as spirit? How well do we know others as spirit? To the extent that we know others and ourselves as spirit, we know God. We can even be so busy trying to learn about God, discovering great revelations and filling our minds with knowledge, we miss our true communion with God. We must take time to go *within* and find ourselves. Remember; *As we find ourselves, we find God.*

As we begin to know God, ourselves, and others as spirit, we start to *live* in the true kingdom of God, which flesh and blood cannot inherit. As we realize that we are God-spirit, we live, move, and have our being in the reality of truth.

Many of us have long held the belief that someday Jesus would come back to earth by appearing before us in his literal body. We have believed the graves in the cemeteries would then open and the bodies would be resurrected and judged. This is a belief religion has created and we have accepted as truth. The true resurrection has nothing to do with this type of scenario.

> "But some may ask, how are the dead raised? With what kind of body will they come? How foolish! What you sow does not come to life unless it dies. When you sow, you do not plant the body that will be, but just a seed, perhaps of wheat or of something else. But God gives it a body as he has determined, and to each kind of seed he gives its own body. All flesh is not the same… there are heavenly bodies and there are earthly bodies; but the splendor of the heavenly bodies is one kind and the splendor of earthly bodies is another. The sun has one kind of splendor, the moon another, and the stars another; and each star differs in splendor. So it will be with the resurrection of the dead. The body that is sown is perishable, it is raised imperishable; it is sown in

dishonor, it is raised in glory, it is sown in weakness, it is raised in power; it is sown a natural body, it is raised a spiritual body." I Corinthians 15:35-44

This passage from I Corinthians clearly tells us the body that is sown is not the body that is resurrected. Within the natural body exists the spiritual body. When the natural body dies, it goes into the earth, the spiritual body is resurrected and raised into the spiritual world. The only body that knows dishonor, corruption or weakness is the natural body. Why would it be necessary for the natural, or physical, body, to rise from the grave? There is no purpose in returning and taking the same physical body again. The spiritual body is immediately resurrected at the time of death or transition. Those who have left the physical realm are not waiting for their old body to be resurrected. The spiritual body is eternal and cannot be destroyed through what we call death. Scientists have proven when a limb of the physical body has been amputated, the outline of the limb can still be seen under certain types of ultraviolet light.

We have a natural body and a spiritual body. In the resurrection, the spirit is resurrected out of the natural body. As the curtain is drawn, we will look into the spirit world and see there is life and movement, which knows no limitations.

If we consider the fact there has been life on earth for millions of years, we must realize how many people have inhabited this planet! It has been said that if all people who ever lived in a physical body were resurrected back into the same body of flesh, they would be stacked up seven miles high around the earth! There is simply not enough room on earth for the billions of people who have died to return to their physical bodies at the same time.

Consider the problem we find in the twentieth chapter of Luke. Two sects, or denominations, were discussing the resurrection. There was a woman who had been married to seven brothers, and the question was asked, "In the resurrection, whose wife is she?" If we choose to believe all bodies are going to be resurrected from the cemetery, many problems would develop at the resurrection. Many people have had more than one spouse. Imagine the confusion when the decision has to be made as to which spouse one would stay with in eternity! This may seem a strange thought, but it is a valid thought if we are to look at the resurrection with a literal interpretation. Now, whose wife would the woman be? Jesus answered them by saying those who live in the external, physical consciousness are the ones concerned with marriage. Those who obtain the resurrection are not concerned with these fleshly things. Those who cross into the spiritual world, either by death or translation, do not live in the same consciousness as those who are in the physical form. They have entered a place in which they know the seriousness of spiritual progression.

We must allow our consciousness to be raised from the limitations of seeing things only in the realm of fleshly existence. Our time spent in mortal bodies is but the beginning of God's plan for the ages. Once we pass from the realm of our fleshly existence, we begin to understand that the spirit is the key to attaining complete and total resurrection. When we leave the natural realm, our spirit takes on a life in the spiritual world at the same level of consciousness we had before leaving the physical world. As the spirit world becomes the controlling factor, we will see dramatic changes enter into the physical world. "God's will shall be done on earth as it is in heaven."

The First Resurrection

The Bible also tells of a *first resurrection* in Revelations 20:4-6:

"I saw thrones on which were seated those who had been given authority to judge. And I saw the souls of those who had been beheaded because of their testimony for Jesus and because of the word of God. They had not worshipped the beast nor his image and had not received his mark upon their foreheads or their hands. They came to life and reigned with Christ a thousand years... **This is the first resurrection**. Blessed and holy are those who have part in the first resurrection. The second death has no power over them, but they will be priests of God and of Christ and will reign with him for a thousand years."

The word *resurrection* comes from the Greek word *anastasis*, meaning *standing up again, raised to life again, and recovery of spiritual truth*. The word *first* comes from the Greek word *protos*, meaning *foremost in time, place or order*, from the root word *pro* meaning *superior*. In the above Scripture, we see the reward for those who attain the first, or superior, resurrection. Each of those who qualify will sit in a place of authority (upon a "throne") where they will be qualified to give righteous judgment to both men and angels as does God. In other words, they will be qualified to judge both spiritual and natural matters.[10] Those who are of the first resurrection are those who overcome traditional religious doctrines of man, which deny the power of God within us.[11] They overcome the realms of religious thinking. The definition of *overcome* is defined as a means of success to victory. We shall be *fully successful* in all that God is by overcoming religious thinking and following the inherent intelligence within!

We see the path of preparation for those who attain this first resurrection. Their souls are "beheaded" externally, for the witness of Jesus and, internally, for the word of God. These "overcomers" have been under tutors and governors[12] representing the heads of the religious system, until the time appointed for their beheading, or *separation*, from the popes, bishops, and pastors of lower orders of Truth. This is the external beheading for the witness of Jesus. They are no longer seen in the fleshly gatherings of man-made religions but are caught up in the General Assembly of the Firstborn[13] (*prototokos*[14]) whose Bishop and Shepherd is Jesus Christ.[15] These people are now with the Lord but no longer call him Lord—they call him Ishi or Husband.[16] This concept

---

10   I Corinthians 6:2-3
11   Revelation 2, 3
12   Galatians 4:2
13   Hebrews 12:23
14   *From this Greek term we get the English word: prototype.*
15   I Peter 2:25
16   Hosea 2:15

of marriage demonstrates the need for balance between the masculine and feminine energies. There are two energies that exist within our being, the male and the female, the yin and yang. Men must discover and become comfortable with their feminine aspects. In the same respect women need to discover their masculine aspects and become comfortable with them. Jesus is a perfect example of balancing these energies. He was comfortable with his feminine aspects in which He displayed publicly.

The second aspect of "beheading" is internal and begins with a union or marriage with the Lord[17] as they begin to *know* God in a new and different way. This knowing is intimate, such as the relationship of marriage. It is a union that produces manifestation. As these "overcomers" unite in an intimate union with the Lord, they are prepared for the power of the first resurrection.[18] They begin to know Christ within. This internal "beheading" brings separation from the ego's perception of the world governed by the five senses and initiates the relationship with the spiritual world that cannot be externally discerned.

They do not worship the beast nor receive his mark upon their foreheads (in their minds) or hands (their ways). The beast is the system of religion that keeps man at the tree of knowledge of good and evil where he continues to focus on death and fear instead of life and the love of God. The focus of the beast is the duality of good and evil. As we release ourselves from the teachings that have held man captive in this duality of good and evil, we are refusing to take the mark of the beast! Any belief, which keeps man separate from the knowledge of his indwelling Christ, will be consumed by the brightness of the Christ consciousness appearing within.[19] Those who attain the superior resurrection will lose their lives, or lose their false sense of self—the life that is governed by the external world.

What is the resurrection? The resurrection is *the recovery of truth*. Those who attain the first, or superior resurrection while yet in a physical body will attain it through truth. To recover (re-cover) something, you must first have had it to have it again. It matters not whether in the body or out of the body, there is a trumpet sounding that is bringing

---

17   *Isaiah 62:5*
18   *Philippians 3:10-11*
19   *II Thessalonians 2:8*

the recovery of truth in both the natural and spiritual worlds. Hebrews 11 tells us the saints of old, those heroes of faith, cannot be made perfect without us. Their perfection will be complete through a word that will be brought forth through those destined to be in the earth in this day. It is the day of the Lord, a day such as has never been before. This simply means it is a day of total *recognition* of truth as we turn to the Christ *within*. Those who have left the physical realm attained **a** resurrection, but not **the** resurrection. As truth is restored and the trumpet sounds, those with ears to hear, in both worlds, are awakening and remembering.

The superior resurrection is the raising of mind and body from physical sense consciousness to spirit consciousness. The resurrected will attain the fullness of Christ that dwells within us. This recovery of truth, or resurrection, occurs when we surrender the veil of our human identity and allow our spirit to be our consciousness. In this space, we are resurrected, and we bring to ourselves our own judgment. We remain aware of how our actions affect others and we judge with our hearts. It is a total dependence upon the indwelling Christ alone that will bring change, for He said, "I am the resurrection and the life."[20] This resurrection is not somewhere in the future, but can be today, as we walk in the reality of the I AM, here and now.

In the I AM reality, we view all conditions and events through the eyes of love. This does not mean we have to condemn another or be condemned ourselves. When we judge righteously, through the eyes of love, we choose to love unconditionally and to see that in all things lies the presence of God. We judge that all things are evolving on their own path and in their own space and time. We can view all events as neutral for there is no reason to fear—no harm can be brought to the truth of who you are when you accept the knowledge of yourself as a spiritual entity. This is why Jesus could withstand the crucifixion and forgive his persecutors while still in a physical body—no harm was brought to the entity that is the Christ. Likewise, no harm can be brought upon anyone who is in the reality of their true identity, or Christ-self.

> "Who has saved us and called us to a holy life—not because of anything we have done but because of his

---

[20] *John 11:25*

> own purpose and grace. This grace was given us in Christ Jesus before the beginning of time, but it has now been revealed through the appearing of our Savior, Christ Jesus, who has destroyed death and has brought life and immortality to light through the gospel." II Tim. 1:9-10

What a powerful Scripture! Saved and called with a holy calling— not by our works, but by God's grace and purpose which we were given before we ever came to the earth. Notice, life and immortality are brought to light through the gospel. The word *light* means *to illuminate, shine, make to see, or make manifest.* The *gospel*, or good news, is *truth in its purity*, illuminated by the indwelling Christ. With the reality of the indwelling Christ at hand, immortality manifests. With the illumination of the Truth, the whole man is lifted into Christ consciousness. This change is a daily process in which the power of God consumes our belief in the power of death. "The wages of sin is death" and "whatsoever is not of faith is sin".[21] In medieval terms, the Greek word for sin is *hamartano* or, in English, *archery* which means *to miss the mark*. *Mark* comes from the word *charagma*, or *character*. Missing the mark is **missing the true nature of who we are**. As we allow the faith of God to flood our being and know that our calling is by purpose and not by works, we stop trying to please God in the flesh. Instead, we allow God to live *through* us as us. We allow the flesh to be aligned to its true spiritual purpose. This is what it means to be raised into Christ consciousness; it is the manifestation of the whole-- spirit, soul and body.

> "Marvel not at this: for the hour is coming, in that which all that are in their graves shall hear his voice, and come forth: they that have done good, unto the resurrection of life; and they that have done evil, unto the resurrection of damnation." John 5:28-29

Here is an example of the raising of our consciousness. All that are in their graves shall hear the voice of the Son and come forth. When

---

21   *Romans 6:23; 14:23*

we hear the word *grave*, we immediately associate it with a plot in a cemetery. But the word *grave* is from the Greek, meaning *remembrance*. It comes from the root word *mimnesko*, which means to *recall to mind*. Another form of this same word is *mnaomai*, meaning a *fixture in the mind, mental grasp, or to remember*. To be resurrected from the grave, means to recover all that is stored in the memory of the Christ mind, but has been forgotten by the individual mind. *The grave is the realm of lost truth.* It is the darkened mind, or fallen state. Many call this the dark side of the soul.[22] Who needs a voice to sound in their graves: those who wait for bodies to literally arise from earthly graves, or those who wait for a rapture and blame the devil and damn men to hell as an insurance of godliness? The latter are the real dead—they are in the *grave*, dead to the truth as they walk in physical bodies. *All* shall hear the Voice of the Son! The word *hear* means *to understand,* and the word *voice* means *a language or tone*. There is a voice sounding forth a certain language, yesterday, today and forever. It is the language of the spirit. When the darkened mind begins to *hear with understanding*, it is immediately resurrected. The scripture says that the moment is coming when all who are in their graves shall hear (understand) a voice and be resurrected. It does not matter that only a few are hearing at this time. That number is picking up momentum and soon ALL shall hear! As you hear the voice and open the darkened recesses of the mind, all former truth is restored. You look to the inner Christ who is the Alpha and Omega of the spirit, soul and body of every being on the earth. Those who are resurrected behold the Christ within and release the "sinner-saved-by-grace" consciousness and allow the inner man to be given life and movement. This brings full salvation and deliverance to their own soul and body.

> Marvel not at this: for the hour is coming, in the which all that are in the graves shall hear his voice, [John 5:28]

> And shall come forth; they that have done **good,** unto the resurrection of life; and they that have done evil, unto the resurrection of damnation. [John 5:29]

---

22   *Ephesians 4:18*

> I can of mine own self do nothing: as I hear, I judge: and my is just; because I seek not mine own will, but the will of the Father, which hath sent me. [John 5:30]

Consider the two realms of resurrection as spoken in John 5:28-29: the resurrection of life and the resurrection of damnation. The word *good* means *intrinsic, the characteristic of the material itself, the essential nature and not the contents of any impurities it contains*. The word "good" does not imply an attainment through self-works or outer effort. It speaks of the reality of which a person consists -- without the consideration of impurities or hidden defects. To know the reality of a person, one must go beyond the external form to the essence of God, which is in all. Those who attain the resurrection of life do so by viewing all things from the essence of what it is, without attaching impurities.

The word *damnation* comes from the Greek word *krisis* meaning *judgment or condemnation*. The evil that is resurrected will be brought to a place of righteous judgment that brings correction. In the original language, the word *evil* means *foul, to clog or obstruct with a foreign substance, to disrespect or discredit*. It also means a flaw, which is a hidden defect that may cause failure under stress or weakness. Those who are resurrected in judgment have only dealt with the outer person. To focus only on the outer person clogs and obstructs the flow of God's life and brings dishonor and disrespect to the true essence of the person-- the spirit. If we do not consider the Christ within, and see only the weakness of the flesh, we are viewing the foreign substance and not the true substance.

Within each of us is good and evil. But the only thing that brings evil to manifestation is dwelling on the foreign substance or impurities. As we focus upon the life of the Christ within, the Christ will increase and the impurities decrease.

> He must increase, but I (ego) must decrease. He must grow more prominent, I (ego or impurities) must grow less so. (John 3:30 Amp.)

As the voice of understanding speaks, we see evil brought to judgment as we deal with those things hidden away in the mind-- the grave. Events of the past that have harbored in the subconscious mind, which have created resentment and fear, will be dispelled as they are brought to light by truth. Those who are in the grave, bound by the darkness of the mind, will hear the voice. Two degrees of resurrection can take place. We will either look at the impurities or look past the impurities to the true nature and behold the pureness of the spirit. If you refuse to look at spirit, insisting upon beholding the weaknesses of the flesh, you choke, clog, and obstruct the flow of life until you remain in captivity. When you focus on spirit, all things are resurrected. All that is evil will be raised to a higher vibration and will no longer be manifested in your life. We must be resurrected to look past the flesh, to know no one by the flesh but to know the Christ in everyone. This resurrection does not occur by trying to live a life for God-- we have tried to live a life for God for thousands of years and it has not worked! It cannot be produced by fleshly efforts-- we must *allow the Christ to live a life **through us***. Psalms 17:15 tells us that while in the flesh, we are asleep, but we can *wake up* and know that we are like God. "As for me, I shall behold thy face in righteousness: I shall be satisfied, when I awake with thy likeness."

The Spiritual and Natural Worlds Coming Together

We must tear down the walls in the mind that separate spirit from the natural world. God brings forth a word to those who have left the physical body and to those who still have a physical body. This will bring the two worlds together, so they will literally be able to commune with one another. This is not in reference to séances, etc. but to the fact that physical bodies are being attuned to such a high frequency that we are able to quicken them to the same frequency of the spirit realm. Some believe when Jesus left the earth realm that he went somewhere out into outer space. On the day of Pentecost, he walked through the wall of flesh, into the heavens, and presented his life, in the symbol of his blood, to the father in the realm of the spirit as the Holy Spirit. When Jesus walked through literal walls before his ascension, he was not trying to do some supernatural thing to start a miracle revival center. He was exhibiting principles pertaining to the kingdom, proving although he took on a physical form, he could walk through matter.

Creation was originally lowered from the spiritual realm to the flesh realm. In the Son's journey to re-enter the heavens, he will have to go through the flesh realm. These heavens have received him until the time of the restitution of all things spoken by the mouth of the prophets[23]. As spirit seeks truth, the Christ will come out of the heavens and walk into the mind, to finally walk into the flesh and illuminate every cell and atom of the physical body. Mortality will be swallowed up in light. Where does all of this come from? Out of you! Out of me! Out of your innermost being, rivers of living waters shall flow! This will be the greatest baptism man has ever known. We have gone down in literal water under every formula possible, but this baptism will be the immersion of the outer body into the river of the inner Christ.

Jesus learned how to re-pattern the molecular structure of his body by raising the vibratory frequency of his cells, hence – the resurrection. In the physical realm we are learning to make our body become spiritual so we can go into the spiritual world, appear, and reappear from natural to spiritual. Those in the spiritual realm are learning how to come into the natural realm, appearing and reappearing from one side to the other. The veil between the worlds exists only in the mind. As we understand the veil can be lifted, there is no need for us to desire the return of our loved ones into their physical bodies so we may have communion with them. Great mysteries are being revealed in both worlds that will bring the two worlds together. Before there can be a counterfeit there must first be the real process. We have heard many theories that make us fear the opening of our minds. When we lose our fear through the understanding of truth, we experience entering the great and mighty day of the Lord.

We are to know no man after the flesh, even in the physical form. When we no longer know each other by the flesh, we will know each other by the spirit. We will then know everyone on the same level.

---

23   Acts 3:21

If we can know someone by the spirit who is on earth in the physical body, then why can't we know someone by the spirit in the spirit world, who has no physical form? There is a host, or cloud, of witnesses all around us. Each time we gather and truth is proclaimed, this spiritual host hears the same word that brings salvation to both worlds. It is a tremendous experience when the veil lifts and there is communication between the natural and spiritual worlds.

We must become God's spiritual availability. We, as spiritually awakened people in a physical form, must allow God to be revealed out of the heavens and into the physical realm. We must not fear the invisible any longer. We fear it only because our spiritual eyes are closed. Did not Elijah ask God to open the eyes of his servant that he might see the heavenly host all around? As we remove the limitations of our thinking and dare to step out into truth, we will find all we have desired to see is around us.

WHAT DOES HINDER THEE?

Reality vs. Unreality

"Ye did run well; who did hinder you that ye should not obey the truth?"[24]

Ignorance is the greatest enemy of man.[25] It is the cause of poverty, famines, disease and the dark conditions of the world. Yet, we repeatedly blame God for this. Why? We forget God placed the power to create within his creation - man. It is man, with this creative ability and free will, who is responsible for the conditions of the world. He produces, or creates, from the level of consciousness that he has acquired. It is his God-given ability.

God's will shall be done in the earth as it is in the heavens. This won't be accomplished through robots, void of the freedom of choice, but through people who transcend human consciousness. This will be accomplished through people who awaken to a God consciousness with the ability to recreate a world of peace and harmony.

In Psalms 82, we find God judging among His gods (the Elohiym[26]). He asks the question:

---

24 Galatians 5:7 KJV
25 The Sanskrit word for man is "manas" which means "mind" or to think. Therefore, man's ability to create his world by his thinking.
26 gods, in the ordinary sense – of the supreme God. Occasionally applied by way of deference to magistrates. (representatives) gods, goddess.

> "How long will you judge unjustly, and accept the persons of the wicked? Deliver the poor and needy: rid them out of the hand of the wicked... all the foundations of the earth are out of course. I have said, Ye are gods; and all of you are children of the Most High, but ye shall die like men... Arise, O God, judge the earth: for thou shalt inherit all nations."

This particular passage of Scripture provides amazing insight into Truth. We see God place the responsibility of humanity upon the Elohiym. He does this because the Elohiym chose to come to earth for the purpose of setting its foundations back on course. It is time to shake ourselves from the dust of the confusion of humanity and stand in the earth as saviors for mankind.[27] All of creation is groaning and travailing for the manifestations of the children of God.[28] We must find that which has hindered us from allowing God to be present *within* us. Divine manifestation can only come as we allow "The Son" to manifest His nature through us. The weights that have so easily beset us are not a part of our reality as we live in the life of God.

We must become co-creators of peace and harmony within our own worlds and then we will have the power and the ability to reach out to the ends of the earth and the universe, bringing reconciliation to all.

The Elohiym are responsible for creating a new age on earth. *You* are responsible for creating a new age on earth; it is your divine responsibility. How do we fulfill our responsibilities as Elohiym? It is through the shifting of our perceptions, and changing the way we think and view the world. By this we change its reality. Every thought must be of the indwelling Christ. "Let this mind be in you which was also in Christ Jesus."[29] This demonstrates that the indwelling thoughts of spirit overshadows the thoughts of the ego mind. You must release your thoughts and perceptions to spirit so they will manifest divine order. Your thoughts, which are validated by your own belief system, will eventually be made manifest. We believe there is crime and poverty, and so it is. We believe there is sickness and death, and so it is. We empower these conditions with our belief and acceptance of them!

---

27 Obadiah 1:21
28 Romans 8:22
29 Philippians 2:5

This is the day of the Lord. That day is a time of total recognition of who we are, where we came from, our purpose for being on the earth and where we are going. Many ideas in the physical realm that appear to be monumental, will literally crumble before you as you return to the realm of God consciousness, leaving all influences of humanity in the realm of dust. The day of the Lord is a time of total recognition of who we are and where we have come. It is recognizing our purpose for being on the earth and understanding the purpose can be fulfilled. The Elohiym have gone to sleep in human thought and form, but are now awakening and remembering the fullness of all spiritual blessings once experienced before the foundations of the earth.[30]

The Realm of Appearance

The word *appearance* means *outward aspect, external show, view or form*. The realm of appearance is in the realm of the five senses. It is based on what one can see, hear, touch, taste, and smell. To live in the realm of appearance is to judge things after the flesh or from a human point of view. The Scriptures speak to us concerning the realm of appearance:

> "Abstain from all *appearance* of evil." I Thessalonians 5:22

The word *evil* comes from the Greek word *poneros* meaning *hurtful, diseased, guilt, devil and sinners*—all of these are referred to as being an *appearance*. What an amazing thought! The things that create pain and grief are only appearances! They are not a part of our reality. Our belief in evil is a belief in an appearance. We have been programmed to believe evil is reality and the opposite of good-- remember "evil" is "live" spelled backwards. Evil belongs in the realm of appearance and is not

---

30 Ephesians 1:3-4

a part of the realm of reality. The fruit of both good and evil produces the same effect; death, which is a part of our duality thinking.

If we took a survey among fundamental Christians, most would say the opposite of God is the devil. Many picture God and the devil as equal powers in opposition to each other. In truth, God the Creator, and the devil the created, cannot exist on the same level. Religion has presented the illusion of a war between God and the devil. Sometimes God wins, sometimes the devil wins. Some days God has control, other days the devil is in control. Man pleads with God so he may remain free of the devil and his temptations. Humanity lives in endless struggles while declaring God omnipresent. This is duality thinking.

God is omnipresent and there is no other. God is not at war with the devil or anything else. It is only man's thoughts that create an appearance of the devil. It is man's *belief* in the appearance of evil that creates evil. The battle with the mind will continue until we realize that the Creator and the Created share the same level. God inhabits eternity and is God's own fulfillment. God is the totality of beingness. The only opposite of God is God! How can God have an opposite if God is omnipresent? From His right hand are eternal pleasures[31] and from His left[32] hand are the songs of love, which guide the evolving soul.

To know the reality of something, we must be able to identify its source. In our duality thinking, we consider the opposite of day to be night. The source of day is the sun. Day is a reality for we can find its source. What is the source of night? It has no source. Night is only the *absence* of light. Night is an appearance. When one side of the earth moves away from the sun we call it night. Day does not stop; it is present on the other side of the earth.

What is the night of the mind that creates the appearance of evil? It is only the absence of knowledge and the understanding that God exists in all things. Night is not reality; it is only the absence of reality. People want to fight darkness by casting the devil of darkness out. The only way to expel darkness is to be in the reality of light. Turn the light on! Darkness does not go anywhere because it never existed. Darkness is only a vacancy, an appearance. Once light or truth comes, it fills the vacancy. Try to fill a container with darkness. The minute you take it into the light, it no longer exists. We cannot bring darkness into light,

---

31 Psalms 16:11
32 Strong's Concordance: Hebrew "Zamar" to celebrate in song & music.

but we can bring light into darkness. Again, be it hurt, disease, guilt, the devil, or any form of evil, the vacancy can be filled with enlightenment and understanding. Enter this realm of reality, past all appearance of evil, and *be the Light* that you are. It will no longer matter what is happening around you, the light radiating from you will eliminate all the evil and darkness that you once considered reality. People will be changed by your very presence. You will know and understand all manifestations of the appearance of evil are only containers of darkness. The light in you overcomes all darkness!

> "Yea the darkness hideth not from thee, but the night shineth as the day, the darkness and the light are both alike to thee." Psalm 139:12

Only man lives in the consciousness of light *and* darkness. God tells us it all looks the same. It matters not what you see, or what *appears* to be happening in your external world. All that matters is where you stand in consciousness. It is through consciousness we cease to discern things around us as good or evil, day or night. Treat people as they appear to be and they will remain so. Treat people as they are to become, in the light of knowledge and understanding, and they will become whole and complete -- not according to the standards of the world, but according to God's standards. You are a child of God. It is a disservice to the Divine for a child of God to live in darkness and fear! Every one is searching for their source and the source of every one is God! Carl Jung, the great psychologist, defines darkness as being "our unconscious light". What we call darkness is really a place where our *light is absent from our consciousness*. As we leave the realm of the appearance of darkness, we become a light in the earth. We join the Great Light in a participation to swallow up all darkness!

> "Judge not according to appearance, but judge righteous judgment." John 7:24

I once held a picture of a landscape before an audience, pointed to part of it and asked what it was. The response was: it was a tree. I asked the person who identified it as a tree to pick a leaf from the tree and give it to me. The mind was shocked from *appearance to reality*. The *appearance* was that of a tree, but the *reality* was, it was only a picture, or image, of a tree. The mind usually does not perceive things in reality, but judges things to be real according to how they appear externally. As the spirit overshadows the thoughts of the mind, which judge externally and by appearances, all thoughts transmute into a higher order. As you leave the realm of appearance, evil takes on a different form. It is not seen as wicked and sinful; but is recognized as an *undeveloped good*. We need to re-educate ourselves-- to give love, patience, and understanding freely to the world. We need to develop our good, allowing our eyes to see beyond the realm of appearances and into the heart, or true essence, of all.

> "...The Lord seeth not as man seeth; for man looketh on the outward appearance, but the Lord looketh on the heart." I Samuel 16:7

When we look to the heart, or essence, of all, we see as the Lord sees. Traditions and doctrines have made the scriptures ineffective. We have insisted upon working our way into the kingdom of God through external means instead of being in the kingdom. Paul tells us in Corinthians that the realm of appearances is temporal:

> "While we look not at the things which are seen, but at the things which are not seen: for the things which are seen {are} temporal; but the things which are not seen {are} eternal." II Corinthians 4:18

In this scripture, the things that are seen are those viewed in the realm of appearances. Paul tells us that these things are temporal. We are so physically conscious, we judge everything in the realm of the physical form. If those things, which can be seen, are only temporal, then we must consider them an illusion. Webster defines *illusion* as *perception of something existing in such a way as to cause **misinterpretation** of its actual nature*. We are spirit, the offspring of God. In the reality of this realm exists all things which are eternal and cannot be seen. The answer to the question, "what does hinder thee?" lies in the conscious awareness that our true essence is merely separated by the illusions and appearances of humanity. When we see in the eternal realm, we deny separation. We live in the *eternal* true essence of our beings.

When Jesus spoke of "this world", he spoke of the physical, and external, temporal realm of existence. Because the material sense of the universe is an illusion, Jesus was able to overcome to the point that even the elements of nature were subject to him. Jesus knew which is reality and which is illusion. When he came upon the blind, deaf and lame, he saw past the external appearance of their physical limitations and into the reality of their spirit. Miracles are only supernatural to those who judge by appearances. When we are able to look past physical conditions and see the reality of spirit, we will literally revolutionize the world. The only way to overcome the world of lack and limitation is to know the conditions of the physical are only illusions existing in the realm of appearance.

Each person born into the human race has come under some kind of hypnotic spell. We perceive the external, physical manifestations as reality. This is a universal, hypnotic spell that takes on many forms. We know it as disease, poverty, drug and alcohol addiction, sexual issues, and so on. In order to be released from this spell, we must bring the axe to the root of the tree. We have spent far too much time trying to pick off the branches. It does not serve us to engage in a little healing here or there; we must get to the root of the problem and know we are dealing with an inner condition and not just the outer actions of the individual. Behind every fault and failure, there is a cause. This knowledge is our only hope of escape. We must turn to the indwelling Christ, allowing Christ thoughts to flow through us in a way that transforms life as we have known it. Only the thoughts of the indwelling Christ can take our thoughts of appearances and deliver us from all illusions.

God told Abraham to look at the sky and see the multitudes of stars as God's seed, which would come through Abraham's loins.[33] Had Abraham judged things by appearances and not by the reality of the word of God, those words would never have been fulfilled. Abraham looked at those stars and called things which were not as though they were. By the faith of God, he became the father of many nations. Past the realm of appearance there is great potential for manifestation. The

---

33 Genesis 15:5

power of the creative word that springs forth from an inner awakening will create new worlds of reality. That which appears to us as the mere temporal existence of everyday life, can be transformed into the reality of the eternal. Manifestation is not something made out of nothing. It is taking what you already have and transforming it into another level. We must be able to look past the realm of appearance of any situation and see its hidden potential. Sometimes, what we appear to have may not seem like much, but *within* is the potential of the very thing we are seeking. By learning how to activate any given situation with a creative word, we can literally transfer it from one glory to another and change the nature or character of that situation. This will never be done while looking at the external appearance; in that realm, things *appear* to be hopeless and impossible. Limitations vanish and illusions become unreal for those who will step beyond the boundaries of appearances.

How many times have you experienced sickness or some other situation in your life in which you refused to acknowledge it with your words, but the situation did not get better? "With the heart, man believeth unto salvation and with the mouth confession is made unto salvation" (Ro.10:10) Until the change takes place within, it does not matter what you confess with your words. When you are sick and say, "I am whole", when you are having financial problems and say, "I am prosperous", when anything in physical manifestation is out of alignment and you confess the situation is corrected, that confession is not reality. It will not bring deliverance until you know you are speaking out of the true *essence* of your being, not from the carnal (ego) mind. This is not mind over matter. It is knowing who you are and living in that consciousness. Salvation will then move from spirit into the mind to become a creative thought. The spirit impregnates the mind with the thought, "I am healed. I am whole". These thoughts are the vehicle of the spirit-- your thoughts become that which the spirit is radiating. You begin to think God's thoughts, tuning your thoughts to a higher frequency, and in the twinkling of an eye, you think as God. This is reality. Illusions and appearances are transformed and become reality! Not by the works of your flesh or mind (ego), but by the effectual working of the Christ consciousness within.

Awakening From the Dream

Science has proven that we all dream at night. Once, I dreamt that I was swimming in a large body of water like an ocean. I had swum out too far and needed help, but no one could hear my cries. As my life flash before me, I could see my parents and my daughter and felt I would never see them again. Suddenly, I awoke to the sound of my telephone ringing. As I woke up, I heard the voice of Spirit say simply, "I want to teach you what a miracle is." Those who receive miracles are awakened to reality. The problems we experience in the physical realm are only as real as the dream that I had of drowning. Awakening to reality is to awake from our slumber in the realm of appearances. We experience the miracle of transformed living when we awake from the dream of our physical existence.

II Corinthians 5: 16 has been quoted many times in the message of reconciliation:

> "Wherefore, henceforth, know we no man after the **flesh**…"

Sometimes, I think we hear certain things so often that we do not *hear* its truth.

The word *flesh* comes form the Greek word *sarx*, meaning *the body, symbol of what is external, human nature, carnally minded*.

> "For to be **carnally minded** is death." Romans 8:6

The word carnally comes from the same Greek word as flesh. We have thought of the carnal mind as something unclean, wicked, evil, and lustful. This is a religious interpretation. The carnal mind is simply a mind that is affected by the external, physical realm of body consciousness. Flesh and the carnal mind are symbols of the external. To live in this consciousness brings death. Webster gives an interesting definition of death: "the *lie* of life in *matter*." This means that as long as we know ourselves after the flesh, we are carnally minded. The death we experience, whether it is sickness, poverty, dysfunctional relationships or addictions, is a *lie*, expressing itself in the physical realm.

How do we stop knowing ourselves after the flesh through the carnal mind? By awakening to the truth that we are spirit, made in the image and likeness of God. As we look past the physical appearance and see ourselves in the reality of our true essence, we will begin to project that kind of thinking. The mind no longer projects itself through the body, but projects itself through spirit. Spirit becomes light running through the mind, or projector, and appearing as the outer conditions of our life.

> "When Christ who is our life, shall appear, then shall ye appear with Him in glory." Colossians 3:4

> "…When He shall appear, we shall be like Him; for we shall see Him as He is." I John 3:2

The appearance of Christ takes place as we recognize our union with Him. As the Christ appears, we appear. We see ourselves in the reality of our true being; the spirit. There are no limitations or illusions of death in the realm of spirit. As we join with spirit in true union, conception occurs, the Christ within overshadows the virgin mind, or soul, and the manifestation is seen and experienced in the body.

Whenever you feel discouraged or depressed, immediately detach yourself from that feeling and know who you are. Close your eyes and visualize a picture of something, anything and realize you are only looking at the picture. You are not the picture. You view things as they go through you. When feelings come, allow them to go through you, remembering the feelings are not who you are. Know as Christ is, you are also. Your mind may not feel so good, but you are not the mind or the thought. Truth coming out of spirit and going into the mind forms a spiritual mind. We are already a spiritual spirit; we are becoming a spiritual mind that we may become a spiritual body.

We were with God before the foundations of the world, and we are with God in the reality of our spirit. Our awakening to this reality is our miracle. It is said life began when we came into the world of matter in a physical body. The opposite is true. When we came into the world of physical matter, we fell asleep in human thought and form.[34] We have been programmed from the beginning of our walk through humanity to have problems, sickness and finally, death. Due to this programming and conditioning, we have forgotten all we once knew in the realm of spirit. The realm of spirit became an illusion and the external world of matter became our reality. The Scriptures speak to us of our own awakening:

> "Awake and sing ye that dwell in dust." Isaiah 26:19

> "Awake, awake, put on strength, O Zion put on thy beautiful garments… Shake thyself from the dust, Arise…" Isaiah 52:1,2

The word *awake* comes from the Hebrew word *quwts*, which means *to arise, spend the harvest season*. Dust is the realm of humanity, knowing ourselves by the flesh or physical form. For everything, there is a time and season. It is not by accident that we entered this world, lost all memory of the spiritual realm and became subject to the illusions of the external realm. For an appointed season, we make our journey through the realm of appearances, through humanity. Our Harvest time has come; *awake*!

We awaken to the light that we are. Romans speaks of our slumber and our return to our "armor of light":

> "Knowing the time, that now it is high time to awake from sleep, for now is our salvation nearer than when we believed. The night is far spent, the day is at hand, let us, therefore cast off the works of the darkness and let us put on the armor of light." Romans 13:11,12

The word *awake* in this scripture is from the Greek word *egeiro*, meaning *to collect your faculties, awake from disease, death, nonexistence and ruin*. This scripture confirms death and disease are but a dream, an illusion, an appearance. It assures us now is the time to put on our

---

34   Genesis 2:21

armor of light, to recognize that the light is our only reality, and to find strength in the light from the appearance of our illusions.

When I awakened from the dream of drowning, a miracle had happened. I awoke to the realization I had only been dreaming of drowning. As we awaken to spiritual understanding, we find things that have been so very real to us were only a dream, a lie in the life of matter. When I was a child, we played a game that held you as prisoner inside chalk marks until someone tagged you and you were set free. One day, the other children decided to play a trick on me. They slipped away to go home, leaving me in my box, waiting to be tagged. I waited a long time and no one came. I didn't want anyone to think that I couldn't play the game, so I stayed inside the chalk marks. Soon, it started to get dark and I was hungry. Still no one came to free me. After awhile, I began to think, "I don't want to play this silly game anymore." So I simply stepped across the chalk marks that had confined me and went home. Those chalk marks are representative of the doctor's diagnoses; all symptoms, feelings of hurt, anger, bitterness and disappointment. When we tire of the game of life enough, we stop playing by its rules. As we awaken, we find that nothing has been holding us prisoner except the games of the world. What does hinder thee? Learn to step out! Know that you are not bound by the rules of this world! This is the day of salvation. We can move out of all nightmares, all chalk marks, appearances and illusions into the reality of Christ.

David was very specific when declaring:

> "As for me, I will behold thy face in righteousness.
> I shall be satisfied when I awake, with thy likeness."
> Psalm 17:15

David was saying, "I don't care what you think or believe, I have come to my own conclusion. *As for me*, I will see the goal before me and nothing will hinder me from reaching that destination." David had reached a place of stability and understanding. He had found his reason for being. Everything he had experienced had brought him to a place of knowing where he stood. "As for me", he went on to say, "I shall be satisfied when I awake in thy likeness." We will never know satisfaction in the realms of humanity. When awakening begins, it can cause separation and hurt. But as we draw closer to home, we become as David. We know there is only one thing that will ever satisfy us, and we will not compromise with anyone or anything that will hinder our journey.

I thank God for the experience of salvation. I was told that I should be satisfied just knowing that I was saved and on my way to heaven. But, I was not satisfied; something within me cried out for more. I went further on my journey and received an experience with the Holy Spirit. I was told this is the greatest thing this side of the rapture and going to heaven. But soon after, that familiar cry began to pull me up higher. A little farther on my journey, someone preached Acts 2:38 and I was baptized in the name of the lord Jesus Christ for the remissions of my sins. What a privilege and a revelation it was to take on His name. I was told that surely, I should now be satisfied. I wasn't. Soon I heard someone preaching the Sons of God message and it touched me deep within. I sat in this message for a few years until I realized as for me, I would never be satisfied until there is a full awakening and I know myself in the image of Christ. Praise God, we are awakening! We are remembering! We are coming to the realization of who we are, where we came from, why we are here and where we are going.

The City is Your Own

I read an account of an experiment conducted with insects accustomed to the freedom of being able to fly wherever they chose. The insects were placed in a large container with a lid and observed for a period of time. At first, the insects tried to escape from the captivity of the jar. After no escape was found, they settled for the limitations of the sealed container and would only fly so high. Their offspring that were born never attempted to go beyond that which they had witnessed of their elders. They were born in a place of limitation and this was all that they knew. After a period, the lid was removed from the container. The insects could have flown to freedom, which was their true nature, but they did not attempt to cross the line of their conditioning.

This is the same condition of the world today. Religion has failed to teach us that two thousand years ago, Christ Jesus "took the lid off" of every limitation. There are no limits for the person who awakens to their own reality.

Overcoming is not a process of changing everyone to think as you think. An "overcomer" is a person who can look at a situation or person and allow that situation or person to not bring up cause for offense. Then and only then will the power to remit sin become a reality.[35]

The spirit knows no limitations! You are not your body-- when the body appears to have a problem, it is merely a wall built by viewing life through external appearances. Never use the term "I am" and associate it with the body. The "I AM" is never sick nor tired! The body may feel sick or tired but the I AM, your true essence, can never be afflicted. By removing ourselves from the appearance of the physical, our priorities change. We arise to the Christ consciousness that knows no boundaries-- no walls!

The children of Israel lived with a promise for hundreds of years. The day finally came when they found themselves face to face with what had only been a promise. Now it was up to them to lay hold upon the provision. They crossed the Jordan and were in the land they had heard of for so long. They soon discerned, as many do today, that just being in the land does not solve everything. Many people think just getting into the messages of life, reconciliation, kingdom, salvation, and sonship, will solve all of their problems. But there are challenges in this land. Challenges help us to grow. Without a challenge, the children of Israel would have entered the land and said "Well, we are here, and all is well." That would have been the ending of this entire story. As it was, they found their land, but they also had to take possession of it. Like the Israelites before us, we cannot simply stand around the edges of the city just because we have crossed the Jordan. Now we must conquer and possess the land. There are giants that must be driven out of the land of promise before we can experience the provision. The problem however, is not the giants, but our perception of the giants.

---

35   John 20:23

Take Another Look

The children of Israel were accustomed to fighting battles the old way from a former dispensation (the wilderness). They had fought battles with weapons and blood was shed. But things changed. Moses died and Joshua rose, representing a completely different realm of leadership. God told the Israelites to look to Joshua; he would bring a new order and teach them how to enter and possess the land. Joshua's ministry would not be of the Law of Moses, but would be of a new order that did not fit any former pattern. The children of Israel were warned, Joshua's order would appear totally ridiculous to the carnal, religious mind.

> "And it came to pass, when Joshua was by Jericho, that he lifted up his eyes and behold, there stood a man over against him with his sword drawn in his hand; and Joshua went unto him, and said unto him, Art thou for us, or for our adversaries? And he said, Nay but as a captain of the Lord of host am I now come..." Joshua 5:13-14

Joshua was met by an angel (a messenger) who drew his sword (the word) and began to instruct him. Since all of this was apparently new to Joshua, he asked the messenger, "Are you for us, or our adversaries?" When people first begin to hear truth from God, they too ask, "Is this truth or are you a false prophet deceiving the people? Who is this messenger who stands with sword drawn before me, challenging all that I have been taught to believe?" The answer that the messenger gave Joshua was, it did not matter how he fought battles under the Law of Moses (the law, former age), things would now be done differently. Under the way of Moses, the fighting would continue forever. Now I will show you, there is no battle, it was only caused by the way you viewed conditions. If I can change your view, you will never again lift a sword to fight another battle."

Are *you* ready to stop fighting and enter God's day of rest?

> "For the children of Israel walked forty years in the wilderness, till all of the people who were men of war, who came out of Egypt, were consumed, because they obeyed not the voice of the Lord." Joshua 5:6

The number forty is symbolic of trials, tests and tribulations. We remain in the wilderness experience until that part of our nature, which insists on fighting battles as a man of war, has died. The message before you today is simple: *do not fight in the battle*. Stand still and see the salvation of the Lord with you... The Lord shall fight for you and *you shall hold your peace*. [36]

Once we enter the land, we must learn how to be more than a conqueror. We can enter the promised land and still be held captive. The Israelites wanted to look at things in the traditional way once they had crossed the Jordan. We see this in the message of reconciliation. A few years ago, I attended a large "Sonship" convention. If I had tuned out to certain words like sonship, life, and elect, I would have thought I was in another old time Pentecostal meeting. God spoke and said, "this is only an attempt to put new wine into old bottles." We must not be guilty of doing the same thing in this the hour in which we live. We need to stop putting new pictures into old frames. We have thought everything we believed had to be in the frame of the Pentecostal, Baptist, and Charismatic style. We want to change the picture, but we also want to hold on to that old frame. We can literally frame new worlds by allowing old patterns to be replaced by the order of today. Are you willing to change your old ideas, point of view and patterns? New wine will burst old bottles. The new will not work in the framework of a passing order. God is bringing forth a word that totally re-educates us to talk differently, and to see all things from a different point of view. The message of today is not another doctrine; but a way revealing life to humanity from a different vibratory level that will cause people to know something is different about you. As this begins to happen, you will not have to go to people, they will come to you, and say, "I don't know what it is you have, but I want it." We are now at a time and place we have never been before. We have passed the order of fighting, judging and condemning.

> "Now Jericho was straightly shut up **because of the children of Israel**... and the Lord said unto Joshua SEE, I have given into thy hand Jericho..." Joshua 6:1-2

---

36   II Chronicles 20:17; Exodus 14:14

In our old way of thinking, we immediately see Jericho as being a problem. We must fight Jericho because it is shut up by walls and men who guard it with weapons. We believe there is no way to take the city without a fight. In truth, there was nothing to conquer concerning Jericho because the city had already been placed in the hands of the Israelites. Notice that the scripture tells us that Jericho was shut up because of the children of Israel. The problem was in the children of Israel, not in Jericho. Jericho appeared to be a problem for them because they chose to see it through their old understanding; therefore, they saw it as being impossible to take without a fight.

The children of Israel were war-conscious, just as we are today. They had been fighting for forty years amongst themselves. They constantly grumbled and complained that nothing was done right. Moses was accused of bringing them into the wilderness to die, which is exactly what happened to the old generation because it was what they feared. They confessed to dying in the wilderness. They blamed Moses when what they had done was bring harm to themselves with their unenlightened attitudes. For thousands of years, we have been as the children of Israel in the wilderness. We grumble and complain, thinking that everything in life is a struggle and a fight. It is not what happens to us in life that causes the battles; it is the way we view what happens.

The messenger said to Joshua, "*See.*" It is time for new insight. It is time to see things from a different point of view and to leave old patterns behind. The realm of appearances looks at the greatness of the city, the soldiers who guard it and the walls around it. The realm of reality looks at the word that declared, "The city is yours!"

The Lord told Joshua that the city had been placed in their hands. All they had to do was encompass the city, the idea, and lay hold on it. You will now pass from the realm of appearance and enter the realm of reality. The process of marching around the city for seven days[37] represents the time it takes for the mind to re-evaluate the realm of appearance and make the shift into the realm of reality. The "battle" of life exists only in the way you view your own understanding. The walls are built because of the way we have been conditioned to believe. The indwelling Christ is our peace and has broken down the middle wall

---

37 *The number 7 represents completeness*

of partition.[38] Every wall and every limitation can crumble-- without a fight. The realm of appearances insists on acknowledging walls and limitations. In the realm of reality, that place of Christ consciousness, you view the same things this time through truth, and a total re-evaluation is made.

Overcoming does not mean to change the world to your way of thinking. An "overcomer" is a person who can look at something from a certain point of view, perhaps be offended at first, but change their point of view until it finds no offense within. Then, and only then, will the power to remit[39] sin become a reality. Nothing offended Jesus. No matter what the circumstance, he viewed all things through the eyes of God and treated them accordingly. As he did, he brought release! He did not get on the same level as sickness or death, he simply said "Arise!" In other words, "If you want to receive deliverance, you must know where I am. Rise, which means to collect your faculties. In doing so, you will know who you are. Understand that you are spirit, created from the mind of God."

The spirit knows no limitations. You are not your body. The body may *appear* to have a problem, but that is only a wall created by viewing things through the external appearance. Never use the term "I am" and associate it with the body. People say, "I am sick." The I AM is never sick! "I am tired," The I AM is never tired! The body may be tired or sick, but the spirit substance that you are, is never afflicted in any way. Once we get past the flesh, and get down to the I AM of ourselves, our priorities will begin to change and we will arise to a Christ consciousness that knows no boundaries or walls. When you arise in consciousness to know that you have come out of God, you will realize, as God is – so you are.

---

38 *Ephesians 2:14*
39 *From the Greek work* aphiemi *meaning to lay aside, omit or put away.*

Beyond Thinking

We have to go through a tremendous re-education process to learn salvation does not come through the works of the flesh. Not only are you not your body, you are not your ego-mind, either. Likewise, salvation is not given through the works of the mind.

> "That you may come to **know**, practically--through experience for yourselves-- the love of Christ, **which far surpasses mere knowledge** without experience, that you may be filled through all your being, unto **all** the fullness of God, that is, have the richest measure of divine presence and become a **body** wholly filled and flooded with **God Himself!** Now to him who by the action **of His power** that is at work **within** us, is able to carry out **His purpose** and do superabundantly, far over and above **all that we dare ask or think**-- infinitely beyond our highest **prayers, desires, thoughts, hopes, or dreams."** Ephesians 3:19-20 Amplified

What a tremendous passage of scripture! To *know* the *love* of God that surpasses all *knowledge*. Knowledge alone has not, and will not, bring manifestation. To *know* is to have a *union* that produces reality. We must *pass* the realm of knowledge and bring it into our experience. To *pass* is to go beyond the usual mark. Knowledge alone will not bring fullness. As we come to an *experience* through *union* with the Christ within, the *whole body, including the spirit and soul,* will be flooded with God!

We have been programmed to believe God's ability to work in our lives was dependent upon our asking for help. "If I can just pray long enough, hard enough, surely I can get God's attention." Are you worn out from being a prayer warrior? The scripture says that God working within, by the action of His own power, is able to carry out His purpose and to do over and above all that we ask or think. What a powerful statement!

> "The Lord said unto my Lord, **Sit** thou at my right hand, until **I make thine enemies thy footstool**." Psalm 110:1

Cease your labors, sit down and let God be God. I am talking about the labors of the mind. We have come past the struggles of works of the flesh, but we still get headaches. We can't sleep at night. Our minds spin in circles as we search to find answers. We are doing the same thing in the mental realm as we have done in the physical realm of works. As long as I work, God cannot. We cannot work simultaneously. As long as I work, I dam up the flow of God. We are so busy trying to make our enemies a personal footstool in the name of God, that He doesn't have a chance at changing the situation. This is harder than laying down the works of the flesh. Have you ever tried to still your mind, to stop thinking? This will be the next step in our journey. As we look at new principles, we will learn how to simply sit down and cease from all mental labors. As we come to the inner knowing, we internalize God and his ability to do far over and above all that we have dared to ask or think. That is powerful!

> "Watch therefore for ye know not what hour your Lord cometh... if the good man of the house had known what watch the thief would come, he would have watched and not have suffered his house to be broken up. Therefore be ye ready, for in such an hour as ye think not the Son of man cometh." Matthew 24:42-44

Look at this passage of scripture symbolically. Matthew 24 was fulfilled in 70 AD. We are not therefore, looking at this from its historical framework, but from what Spirit is saying today. There is something happening in the lives of God's children, but it is not happening in the way that we thought. The scripture says that no man knows the hour of the Lord's coming. Each, as an individual, is waiting and looking for the coming of the Lord within their own being. A specific time or date is not given, but it is when the individual evolves into a certain experience in consciousness.

The thief is positive, not negative, as we may have originally thought. The thief is the Lord, who gave no warning, but came into your house and stole from you your man-made traditions and doctrines that made the Word of God ineffective. Think back to a time in which you had not heard what you hear today. If you had heard some of this back then, you may have closed your mind. You would have been ready when the thief came and he would have taken nothing from you. Be thankful God sneaks in as a thief and, little by little, steals every tradition.

Notice the scripture says the coming of the Son will be "in an hour that you think not". His coming will never take place as long as we are trying to think him into manifestation! Set aside all of the works of the mind. Set aside all of your searching for solutions and answers. Leave the realm of knowledge that makes you think you should have all these answers. The knowledge was to bring you to the place of understanding. In the very moment your mental struggles cease concerning any situation, God will appear and set all things in Divine order.

> "Therefore I say unto you, take no thought for your life, what ye shall eat, or what ye shall drink… Which of you by taking thought can add one cubit unto his stature… therefore take no thought for the morrow."
> Matthew 6:25,27,34

Isn't it amazing and comforting to know that it is not up to you to bring the manifestation of god to pass in your life? By taking thought, we cannot add one thing to our spiritual growth. In the context of this scripture, the birds of the air and lilies of the field were used as examples of the fruit of those who are not consciously working and laboring. The principle is this: those who are not consciously focusing on problems or circumstances find themselves secure and at peace. The mental strain of trying to figure everything out literally stops the whole process of life.

The ability to think is still a useful process. The mind serves its own purpose, but we need to get things into the proper perspective. Within our own thinking process, we take thoughts and produce more thoughts. Thus, our thoughts are not originating from spirit. That is why we sometimes come to that place of feeling "I can't take it anymore!

I don't know what to think!" We are so filled with our own thought processes that we become overwhelmed and find ourselves believing things are hopeless. The minute we learn to stop thoughts and allow spirit to move into the thinking realm, we rise above our own thoughts, desires and dreams.

We rise past all works of the mind and become still in the reality that God is! The moment this happens, spirit begins to move through us in thought and form. Spirit becomes the movement in thought. Thought itself is not the movement, but spirit is the movement within the thought. In our own thought processes, we move thought, which only produces more thoughts instead of bringing solutions. The more we think about something, the more we feel the need to think and the more we think, the more preoccupied we become with it, all of which does nothing but produce confusion and frustration.

> "For thus saith the Lord, the Holy One of Israel, in returning and rest shall ye be saved, in quietness and in confidence shall be your strength…" Isaiah 30:15

Read this scripture carefully. It gives tremendous keys to true salvation and strength. In returning to the consciousness of spirit, we see all things in their finished state. We know before we ever came into humanity, the plan and provision to return to our former estate was placed within, by the power of the indwelling Christ. By entering rest, we cease from our works, in both the flesh and the mind. In the quietness of the mind, all attempts to find answers, by way of our own human ability, ceases. In confidence, we sit down and allow God to work through us, without our help.

In time of quiet, God will manifest. The working mind has hindered us for long enough. Take the time to stop thinking and worrying about everything. Take the time to be without a thought. This may only last for sixty seconds or so at first, but start practicing the art of trying not to figure things out. Stop trying to decide how you will pay your bills, deal with your partner, children, or job--- all those things which appear to be a problem to you. Stop worrying and give no further thought to the situation. The mind is tired and ready to rest. If God is doing something above what we are thinking, then it is time to go beyond our thoughts.

> "Not that I speak from want, for I have learned to be content in whatever circumstance I am in. I know how to get along with humble means, I also know how live in prosperity. In any and every circumstance, I have learned the **secret of being**, filled and going hungry, both of having abundance and suffering need." Philippians 4:11-12 (NASB)

Paul is speaking of a place, or a step, beyond all duality. In this place, you can experience either abundance or lack, but neither is where you are. Enjoy prosperity, survive lack, yet be in neither realm. Embrace the times of blessings and prosperity but do not be shaken if these things do or do not come to pass, because you are not dependent upon either experience. When you come to this place of learning the secret of being, you can view all circumstances and know you are none of these. The secret of being comes when we get in touch with who it is we really are-- our true essence. When you understand that you are spirit, you no longer place your existence upon "things." Speaker Brian Jones once said that we have three types of matter: the matter that surrounds us, anti-matter that science speaks of, and *it doesn't matter*. When we know our true essence, *it doesn't matter* is the reality. The secret of *being* is to not be dependent upon certain things. This is not to say we shouldn't enjoy our "things"; it means that if our "things" are taken from us, it does not matter! "Things" are not the essence of our being. This is the step beyond duality.

What we have asked for from God is far below what God awaits to manifest into our lives. All those things, we have struggled to attain and find answers for, are within our reach. We must simply allow God to be God and work through us.

> "Wherefore I was made a minister, according to the gift of the grace of God given unto me by the effectual working of His power." Ephesians 3:7

We are not to work the ministry; the ministry is to work *through us*. Too many of us seek the things of God instead of the *being* of God. Seek the kingdom first and all of the "things" will be added later.

Perfection cannot be based, or judged, on outward, external things. As long as we believe that, we are separate from our *union* with Christ. "He who is joined to the Lord is one spirit." This is the whole basis of the mystery of the gospel, *Christ in you*, the hope of all glory. People must turn their attention from the body and mind consciousness to stand in their at-one-ment with God, stopping the duality from the realm of spirit. We must realize that it is not me and God, but God as me and me as God. This is union. Union is not one, but oneness. Oneness cannot be Jesus by Himself, or you by yourself. Jesus said He did not want to abide alone, therefore He became the seed, falling into the ground that He might bring forth fruit after His own kind. The world needs to know the Lord. To whom will you point the world? To some mystical person out in the blue skies somewhere? One reason the world does not hear us is because we live a separated life. If you want the world to see the Lord, then be a lord for the Lord to appear through! The world needs to know Christ and they can know Christ through you, the anointed ones.

What does hinder thee? What hinders the salvation of the world? Separation and duality are the gap between the Christian community and creation. We will never reach creation through doctrines and dogma. Each of us must go past the realm of things to manifest God; past all of the efforts of trying to live our lives for God, past all of the knowledge we have about God-- past all of these things—there is a place of union, of oneness, of *reality*.

Hell Yes? Hell No?

History of the Fundamental Doctrine of Hell

If you were to die today, where would you go? Christianity has prompted this question, with its many uncertainties, for centuries. In it lies the depths of our dogmatic fears and our reluctance to think of ourselves as free spiritual beings. The threat of hell as an eternal destination for the "unsaved" soul leads many into a lifetime commitment with fear based religion. Minds are ridden with images of a literal lake of fire and its evil caretaker, who would be happy to have you enter his domain. We have shuddered at the notion of falling into a bottomless pit that burns beings alive throughout eternity. We are reminded of those in hell who wish for ice water but are mocked as they fall to their knees, begging.

Setting our religious fears aside is not an easy thing to do. These fears have been engraved into our minds from years of doctrinal influences and religious teachings. It takes courage to consider the reality of hell—does it exist? Is it possible that thinkers, whom modern Christianity would denounce as false prophets and members of the occult, created the concept of hell in which we have held our faith? How can we free ourselves from a belief system that has used our fear of hell as its driving force? Let us consider the origins of hell's "features".

Western European religious leaders from Roman times, borrowed the doctrines of eternal punishment and torment from the non-Christian

Greek and Roman philosophers. Christianity has assimilated many concepts from earlier religious thought.

The classic writers of the Middle Ages still have a dramatic influence on the Christian world. Their writings and teachings were so well accepted and believed that they became incorporated into the doctrines of the then-existing Church. One of these influential writers was Dante Alighieri (1265 to 1321A.D), who wrote <u>Dante's Inferno,</u> which greatly influenced the Christian doctrine of hell. His other popular book, known as the <u>Divine Comedy</u>, deals with the three levels of hell: hell, purgatory, and paradise. <u>The Encyclopedia Britannica</u> reveres Dante as "one of the towering figures in Western European literature. According to Dante, the visit to hell is an extreme measure, a painful but necessary act before real recovery can begin."[40] Because Dante was considered an authority on his subjects, he had a tremendous impact on society. The fact that he wrote about hell so authoritatively influenced the modern Christians of Rome. However, Dante was not without inspiration; the well-known philosophers and poets Vergil and Plato, whose work was fundamental in molding the Greek philosophy of their time, influenced him early in his writings. Rome later adapted Grecian culture into the Roman Empire and it was for this reason, the Bible was written in Greek.

Vergil, a pagan poet born in 70B.C., was believed by Greek writers and Christians of the Middle Ages to have received divine inspiration to create his work. Although he belonged to the school of pagan thought, Vergil greatly influenced the Greek writers and Christians of the Middle Ages.

Plato, born in 427B.C., was also a pagan Greek philosopher and wrote a book called <u>Phaedo</u>, based on the immortality of the soul. This particular work is where the modern belief of the immortality of the soul originated.

Considering the history, we must accept that many of the general statements by fundamental religions concerning hell originated from the pagan philosophers. Our life long doctrines and beliefs have no root in the Scripture. It is a profound moment in our spirituality when we awaken to the knowledge that many of the doctrines we have accepted come from men who did not use the Holy Scriptures as their source

---

40 *The Encyclopedia Britannica, Volume 16, 15 Ed., pp.971-976*

for inspiration, and subsequent writings. Perhaps it is time to take another look!

What is God's Judgment?

The Holy Spirit is undoing what poor translation has done to the Bible. A great number of people believe that the King James Version of the Bible was written by God and is infallible. We cannot deny the fact that God's Word was indeed perfect and infallible as it was imparted by spirit. However, down through the years, the original manuscript of the Bible has been translated from one language to another. Much of the original text was lost as man inserted words that fit into his particular doctrines and belief systems relevant to that time in history.

The King James Bible would not be respected today, as God's Holy Word by English and American Protestants, if it had not been published under the authority of the King. The Holy Spirit is the author of God's Word and was given to humanity to teach all things. We cannot learn and understand pure Truth by the Biblical text alone. Only the Holy Spirit can reveal pure Truth that has not been tampered with by translators. Using the King James Version of the Bible, Strong's Concordance, along with Lamsa's Holy Bible from Ancient Eastern Manuscripts, enables us to find the original Greek and Hebrew meanings of words. Used properly, with the inherent guidance of the Holy Spirit, this method can begin to undo the harm that has been caused by inferior translations with hidden agendas. It is not necessary to remain in darkness because of the lack of knowledge, which is the principle reason we see the world in such a negative state today. As we open our hearts to the Spirit and allow Him to teach us of the pureness of the Word as it was originally spoken, Truth will make us free and we are released from the chains that hold the religious world captive to fear.

Religion has taught that when an "unsaved" person dies, they go immediately into hell. Have you ever wondered, "Will those believed to be in hell leave to take part in the final judgment, or are they eternally confined to hell and unable to take part in any further resurrection?" What does the Scripture say concerning this? John 5:27-29 addresses this scenario:

> "And hath given him the authority to execute judgment also, because he is the Son of man. Marvel not at this, for the hour is coming, in which ALL that are in the graves shall hear His voice and come forth; they that have done good unto the resurrection of life, and they that have done evil unto the resurrection of damnation."

When reading this passage, recall that the Bible is under the influence of its translators. When the word damnation is used in the New Testament, the original word was *condemnation*. The Scripture refers to the evil being resurrected to this condemnation. The term *evil*, as it is used in the original text, means foul; to clog or obstruct with a foreign substance; to dishonor or disrespect. Likewise, the word *good* means intrinsic, the characteristic of the material itself and not the impurities it contains. When man is separated from the knowledge of who he is (the child of God) and is governed by religious laws of *good* and *evil*, the life flow of God is obstructed by the impurities he sees. This causes him to dishonor and disrespect himself and becomes the only cause of a person being "evil". When one comes to the enlightenment and understanding of who he is, he will begin to focus upon the material itself—that which he is—and not the impurities he discerns in his outer world. This is what causes a person to be "good". It is the state of consciousness a man lives in which creates the manifestation of either good or evil in the outer world. There is no justification for the harm brought to man by holding him in his weaknesses. This only causes the weaknesses to be magnified and manifested into the outer world. Only as Truth begins to turn a person from what he knows as "good and evil" or "right and wrong" can there be a change in the heart of what he is and what he can become on both the physical and spiritual levels. Those who go to a place of correction would do so only because they have not heard the Truth or had the ability to focus on the reality of their true essence as God's children. It is important to know that when the Scripture refers to those who have done evil as being resurrected into damnation, it is not referring to the do's and don'ts of organized religion. What it is referring to is the evolvement of the spirit on the earth plane through the vehicle of humanity.

Any person walking in a physical body on this earth, who has not yet awakened to his true substance, is walking in an "evil" state of consciousness to some degree—no matter how "good' he may think himself. As long as one focuses on the impurities he sees in his life and not upon the reality of his divine substance, there is this element of evil in him that continues throughout his entire life stream.

Those who are "evil" will be resurrected into a place that will cause them to be condemned of who and what they have believed themselves to be, therefore bringing a change into their hearts (repentance) and therefore, turning them to God. Our concept of damnation has been depicted as being without hope; totally damned for eternity. This concept is not presented in the Scripture. When a person is condemned of his "evil" in the true spirit of righteousness, he will awaken and change. Damnation does not mean a final, eternal destiny of punishment and separation from God, but speaks of a process that will bring change. The evils that are resurrected and judged are not at the point of the spirit leaving the body, which we call death. Many of us have been taught that judgment comes immediately after death when one will either go directly to hell or to heaven. This concept has been presented to us as being the judgment of God. However, the Bible does not teach this—It is a doctrine devised from the carnal mind of man. The Bible teaches that ALL men, whether "good" or "evil", shall hear (understand) His voice and be resurrected.

The human mind cannot comprehend the true love of God for it has never known such a love on this plane. Human love is conditional and vindictive. We love on the precept that "I'll treat you the way you treat me and if you do not love me then I will not love you." In this manner, man forever continues to render evil for evil and allows it to run rampant throughout the world. We must learn, as Jesus demonstrated, to overcome evil with good so that we may see a reproduction of God's love manifest in our own human experience.

People who have no "religious" communion with God are accused of rejecting Him. In reality, these people have only rejected the false images presented of God by rejecting a particular doctrine. No one will be able to deny God when His true nature is finally revealed. The Scriptures tell us, "As ALL died in Adam, ALL shall be made alive in Christ, each in his own order."[41] The phrase "in his own order" reveals that salvation is an individual process and not the universal "plan" that we have traditionally called religion. It is the LOVE of God that will bring every man to his resurrection—not the FEAR of God. God is love, and in the scope of His love, he will bring ALL unto Him.[42]

God's Word tells us that as we overcome our "evil" and evolve as spiritual beings on the plane of human existence, we shall sit with Him on the throne. There is proof of this in Revelations 3:21 which says:

> "To him that overcometh will I grant to sit with me in my throne, even as I also overcame and am set down with my Father in his throne."

The "throne" represents the authority to rule. It is not a big chair somewhere in the sky that is large enough for one hundred and forty four thousand "overcomers" to sit on! The throne is symbolic. It represents the people who share in the same authority given unto Jesus, who mastered God's plan of love. We will not be able to live in righteous judgment until we also understand and master God's plan for each of us. Isaiah prophesied of a "branch that would spring forth from the stem of Jessie." Jesus said " I am the vine, ye are the branches." The branch represents the people who, according to the word of Isaiah, will not judge by the sight of their eyes nor reprove with the hearing of the ears, but will judge with righteousness.[43] What is righteous judgment? If God looks upon us with righteous judgment and God is pure love, then simply put, God looks upon us with His heart. *There is no fear in the pure love of God.* God is not interested in the self-righteous works of the flesh, but He is interested in the motive behind our actions. Righteous judgment deals with the inner self, which must first be cleansed so that the outer self may produce the loving righteousness of God. It is in righteous judgment that we are able to look within and

---

41   I Corinthians 15:22-23
42   I Timothy 2:3-9; Titus 2:11; I Peter 2:9; John 12-32; Zephaniah 3:9; Romans 10:13; Jeremiah 31:34
43   Isaiah 11:1-5

find the Christ consciousness and then turn to our brother and see not his "evil" but his Christ consciousness. In this place, we judge with the Divine Order of God. We judge righteously, *seeing only love*, which is all God has ever created us to do and all we are ever truly capable of being. Any belief otherwise is an illusion of religious dogma devised to cause the multitudes to fear God, and to conform to religious order. We must remember that God did not institutionalize religion—man created religion for his own purpose.

A Place of Correction

The English language is vast and complicated. In the translation of the Bible from the Greek and Hebrew languages into English, the context of the original words was lost. A single word in Greek or Hebrew has several different meanings in its English translation. This range of word definition and interpretation has caused the loss of the Truth as it was first given to us by God. In the simplest of terms, translation has led to the misinterpretation of God. To read God's Word and understand it fully, one must be proficient in its original script or be open to discover the effect of the translations on a deeper level. The King James Version of the Bible has many mistranslated words that are misleading to the spiritual seeker. For example, the word *destroy* comes from the Greek word "ollumi," which is from the root of "appollium". This one Greek word was translated into approximately six different English words. In English, each of these words has a distinctly different meaning. Each time the word was translated, the context of the Scripture should have carried through with the meaning of the original word. Consider the use of the word *destroy* in Matthew 10:28:

> "And fear not them which can kill the body, but are not able to kill the soul, but rather fear him which is able to *destroy* both soul and body in hell."

Our English understanding of the word *destroy* gives the meaning of something having no further value. If a person who is evil goes to hell and both their soul and body are destroyed, then the person would no longer exist. From the religious perspective, the person is not destroyed, but lives forever, burning in fire and brimstone.

Now consider the English word *lost* which is derived from the same Greek word that *destroy* was translated from. The English understanding of the words, *destroy* and *lost,* is completely different. Something can be *lost*, but that does not mean that it has been *destroyed*. Look at the word lost as it is used in the passage of Luke 19:10:

> "For the son of man came to seek and to save that which is *lost*."

Just as *lost* is derived from the word ollumi, so is the English word *marred*, used in Mark 2:22. Our understanding of *marred* is to damage or disfigure. It is used in the following passage:

> "No man putteth new wine into old bottles, else the new wine doth burst the bottles and the wine is spilled, and the bottle is *marred*."

Believe it or not, this same Greek word was also translated to *perish*! The English understanding of *perish* is to spoil or deteriorate. It is used in John 3:16:

> "For God so loved the world that He gave His only begotten Son, that whosoever believeth in Him should not *perish*, but have everlasting life."

In one place in the Scripture, the word *ollumi* has been used to present the idea that there is no hope. In another place, it is translated into meaning that Jesus is coming to seek and save those who are lost. The Greek meaning of the word ollumi is *to bring to ruin*. Consider this in the context of each scripture shown. God is able to *bring to ruin*, not torment with eternal punishment both the soul and body. Jesus was sent to seek and save the *lost* sheep, or those who were *in a state of ruin*. He was given to the world that those who would believe in his Truth would be able to escape this place of ruin. The bottles that were marred, or ruined, were of no further use in that condition, therefore they would have to be reprocessed. The son of man came to bring salvation—*or to reprocess*—those *in a state of ruin*. Those who do not know God and do not experience an intimate relationship with Him will be brought to this place of ruin in which His presence is withheld.

Considering this to be the Truth, what is this place of ruin and why would God allow men to enter this state? God has a plan that ultimately leads to the restoration of ALL. The place of ruin is not in having a hardened heart, but in living a life driven by ego rather than God. Man chooses his own state of ruin, by creating a life lived without God at the helm. God does not "hand out" states of ruin to "unsaved" or "lost" individuals. We are solely responsible for the quality of life we live! By living without a God relationship, we choose to reject His love and to accept our state of ruin as our existence. Living in union with God releases the life flow, or the love of God, to manifest itself as your reality. Events that take place from this state of union are seen through the eyes of love. Love is the plan of salvation. It is our universal key to freeing ourselves from hell, the state of ruin. Choosing God is to choose union with the Creator and to forfeit the state of ruin you have created by neglecting the Truth of God. It does not mean there are steadfast rules and regulations one must obey, such as religious dogma suggests. Living in spiritual union with God, there is no need for such rules and regulations, because life force is driven by God rather than by ego. In a life that is God driven, the ego cannot survive, thus ending the dilemma of right and wrong, good and evil, thereby freeing the spirit from its own imprisonment.

The Lake of Fire

Religion has long referred to hell as being an unending lake of fire. However, hell is not a lake of fire! Revelations 20:14 tells us that death and hell were cast into the lake of fire. If hell were such a lake, it certainly could not be cast into itself.

The word *lake* comes from the Greek word *limne*, meaning *the idea of the nearness of the shore*. Another form of this word is *limos*, which means *destitution*. A lake is a *limited body of water or space*. *The nearness of the shore indicates the capability of getting out of the space*. Destitution means *abandonment, deprivation, lacking something that is needed or desired*, and *extreme want*. The lack of those things once possessed and believed to be of greater importance than God will be experienced in this place of destitution. The outcome will be a true realization of the need for God.

The word *fire* comes from the Greek word *pur*, which means *lightning, or the discharge of atmospheric electricity accompanied by a vivid flash of light*. This does not express a body or a lake. The invisible items of God can be clearly seen and understood by items that are visible.[44] The world is full of examples of things taught in the Scriptures. When Jesus spoke with farmers, he used examples such as seeds, and sowing and reaping. When he spoke with fishermen, he gave related examples of fish, nets and boats. Jesus always used those things that were familiar to man when teaching his thoughts. The time has come for us to release our primitive beliefs that have been programmed into us and to discover the true validity of God and His Word.

Out of the concept of fire as lightning, we can now view the judgments of God as being light or truth. The human race has not experienced freedom because Truth has not been taught. The Scriptures speak of those who perish because they do not have a love for truth that may save them. All who do not believe the truth will be damned and sentenced to hell, or a place of correction.[45] Religious minds, void of a love for truth fill the earth today, thus unrighteousness fills the land. Unrighteousness is simply a state of mind in which one does not stand in a right relationship with his Father. This right relationship can only happen with an awakening to Truth, which brings a release from the fear of eternal damnation.

Another form of the word *pur*, from which the word *fire* was taken, is *puroo*, also meaning *to refine*. Jesus made two interesting statements concerning the subject of fire:

---

44 *Romans 1:20*
45 *II Thessalonians 2: 7-11*

"I am come to send *fire* on the earth." Luke 12:49

"Everyone shall be salted with *fire*." Mark 9:49

We must realize that fire originated with God, not the devil. Fire is a symbolic term used throughout the Scriptures that deals with refining and cleansing to create purity.

Another word associated with fire is brimstone. Brimstone comes from the Greek word *theion*, meaning *God-like, divine, and the Godhead*. Both of the words *fire* and *brimstone* come from the root word *theos* meaning the *supreme divinity of God*. Sulfur was sacred to the Greeks and was used to fumigate, purify, cleanse and honor deity. Sulfur was used in the incense offered by the tabernacle priests. It is truly amazing that for centuries we have feared the phrase "fire and brimstone". Religion has used this pattern of fear to hold man in bondage. The dawning of a new day begins as the mind is freed from the chains of religious bondage. One no longer serves God out of fear but out of newfound reverence and respect. God's greatest desire is that men know him in His true nature of love and mercy. God is ever mindful of where His children are and of what is necessary to bring each one to restoration. To be cast into the lake of fire and brimstone is to be cast into God's perfect love in which every man achieves enlightenment.

It is time to be honest and face the facts. Religious scare tactics have not brought the world to salvation. It is time to set aside the primitive doctrines that have taught myths to our children in Sunday School, showing them pictures of a devil with horns, his demons pitching coals into the fire and people screaming in never-ending torture. God has been portrayed as an old man with a long white beard sitting on a throne somewhere up in the sky. These pictures of the devil and hell, God and heaven, are as primitive as the tribal natives who believe it is necessary to sacrifice a newborn child to appease their God.

The original text of the Scriptures says that hell was "created for the devil". God does not deliver any man to hell. He does not decide the judgment that any man enters. Whatever a man sows, that shall he also reap. Every man chooses and creates his own place of judgment and correction—hell, if you please. God does not make the final decision—man does! It is not the will of God that men go through any form of hell to find Him. God's ultimate purpose is for man to come to Him through his own will. Each man has the freedom to choose for himself the direction that will lead him to God.

The deliverance from hell comes to those who allow the process of purification to be completed. Slay your dragons with compassion, love your opposition unconditionally and agree with your adversary quickly. Healing arises out of this attitude.

The Scriptures clearly state that God does not want us to be persecuted under the idea of fear-based religion. Jeremiah 7:31 says:

> "For the children of Judah have done evil in my sight, saith the lord; they have set their abominations in the house which is called by my name, to pollute it, and they have built the high places of Tophet, which is the valley of the son of Hinnon, to burn their sons and their daughters in the fire; which I commanded them not, neither came it into my heart."

We are all familiar with these conditions as they exist in churches today. Man continues to pollute the house of God by making it into a house of merchandise and den of thieves, using his own theories and doctrines to hold masses of people in great fear. If man would dare go into the Word for himself and refuse to listen to the ignorance of doctrines, he would clearly see that it never entered the heart of God to put man into a place of torment and to burn him with literal fire throughout eternity.

Deliverance from Hell

Every time the word hell is used in the Old Testament, it is taken from the Hebrew word "shol", meaning *pit* or *grave*. In the original text, it was not associated with fire or torment. There is not a single instance in which it was referred to as being eternal. In fact, there are Scriptures that express deliverance from hell:

> "For great is thy mercy toward me, and thou hast delivered my soul from the lowest hell." Psalm 86:13

> "The way of life is above to the wise, that he may depart from hell beneath." Proverbs 15:24

The word *delivered* means *to snatch away, to escape,* and *to take out or to rescue*. You cannot be rescued or removed from a place where you are not. Religionists will fight for a hell that burns with literal fire. The Scripture tells us "with every temptation comes a way of escape".[46] It is in hell, the place of judgment and correction, that man learns the folly of his own wisdom and turns to God who is great in mercy and ready to offer restitution.

Psalms 139:8 tells us that if we make our bed in hell, God is there. It does not say that God places us in hell, but if we place ourselves there, He is present. The Scriptures also tell us that if we walk through the valley of the shadow of death to fear no evil, for God is with us.

In II Samuel 22:6 we find David crying out to God that the sorrows of hell, not the torment of literal fire, had compassed him. *Sorrow* means *ruin*. It is the *sorrow* of hell, the *ruin* of hell that causes man to come to the end of himself, and then turn to God. "Thou turnest man to destruction; and sayest, return, ye children of men."[47]

Jonah called out to the Lord from the belly of the whale, which he called "the belly of hell".[48] This is the perfect example of hell as a place where God receives man's attention. Just as Jonah cried unto God from his hell, or place of correction, so shall each man in his own order cry out to God from his own place of affliction and God will hear and deliver.

---

46 *I Corinthians 10:13*
47 *Psalms 90:3*
48 *Jonah 2:2*

David Hulse, D.D.

Appearance of the Anti-Christ

We are in the age of a new millennium. For many, this turn of a thousand years brings religion-instilled fears to the surface regarding how the world (age) will end. Among these fears that religion has taught, is the appearance of an anti-Christ. However, this is not a Scriptural teaching. John says that until we can confess that Christ IS come in the flesh, we remain under an anti-Christ spirit. As you have heard that the antichrist shall come, there are now many antichrists, and by this we know it is the last time.[49] Through these words, we come to understand the anti-Christ was prevalent on the earth before the first century was over—after the death, burial, and resurrection of Jesus Christ.

From its Latin and Greek roots, the word *anti-Christ* means *against* (anti) *anointing* (Christ). The anti-Christ are those who are *against the anointing or the anointed one.* Some teach that the Jewish people are the anti-Christ because they do not believe in the deity of Jesus Christ as the Son of God. Others believe, for different fear-based reasons, that Communists are the anti-Christs. The fact is that none of these people are the anti-Christ that John referred to in the Scripture! The word "anti" also comes from another root word that means *"against"* or that which *stands in the place of* or *instead of.* The anti-Christ's that were on the scene before the end of the first century were those against the true New Testament Church. These anti-Christ's took the place of the headship of the Christ spirit. Until that time, the church only moved by the impetus of spirit. Man did not minister, but *Christ ministered through them.* There was not praise, worship, or singing until Christ moved. Christ was the head of the church. But man began to see the vastness of the New Testament Church as people flocked to it. Under the name of Christ, or the name of the anointing, man began to take over the headship and to do his own work. This is the place religion has rested for over 1900 years. How many churches or denominations actually wait for the leading of the spirit? They simply do not. Men stand in the leadership role with programs and organized religion in hand. They sing and preach *about* Him. They use God's name in

---

49   I John 2:18

countless religious forms. But they know nothing of allowing the spirit to move and direct their services. They honor Jesus as their example of how one should live in relationship to the Father. Jesus, however, said he only spoke those things that he heard his Father say.

The anti-Christ are those who stand in the place of spirit and lead the people through the use of their own egoic mind. Everything is devised by the ego mind rather than by the guidance of spirit. *This is the mark of the beast,* which is the character, or the personality of mankind in the place of the nature of Christ. As long as man devises ideas in his own mind, his own way of doing things, he will carry upon himself the mark of the beast. The word *mark* comes from the Greek word *charagma*, from which we derive the English word, *character*. The mark of the beast is a *character*. It is not a number on your house, license plates, checkbook or credit cards! Men are becoming millionaires writing books about the numbers 666. They do not understand the truth of the "mark" and therefore are not telling people about the "charagma" (nature) of man. It is man's beastly character, which brings only a form of Godliness from a human level. When we are motivated from the character of the spirit, the beastly mark is erased and we take on the mark, or character, of God.

In Colossians 1:26-27, Paul says:

> "Even the mystery which has been hidden for ages, but now is made manifest to his saints. To whom God would make known what is the riches of the glory of this mystery among the Gentiles, which is Christ in you the hope of all glory."

The mystery that Paul speaks of is YOU. *The Christ in you* is the hope of all glory. We must realize that Christ *is* come in the flesh and therefore we are not under the influence of the anti-Christ. We must take a stand against that which is against the indwelling Christ who has come in our flesh. Until we both recognize and accept that Christ is present and has come in the flesh, we will remain under the anti-Christ spirit and attitude, with its hold on mankind. This is the mystery that Paul talks about.

David Hulse, D.D.

The Many Bodies of Christ

I Corinthians 12:12 states:

> "For as the body is one, it hath many members and all the members of that one body, being many, are one body, so also is Christ."

Christ is a singular-compound word. Elohiym, church, and Christ are singular-compound words. Each holds the meaning of being one, yet made up of many. For example: one church, many members; one body, many members; one Christ, many members. This releases us from the fundamentalist idea that the one man, Jesus, is the entire embodiment of the Christ. Religion uses the name of Jesus as if it was his first name and Christ as if it was his last name. Jesus did not ask Peter what his last name was, but he did ask him, "Who am I? Who do the men say that I am?" Peter answered, "Thou art the Christ.[50]" Christ is before the man Jesus and Christ is after the man Jesus. Jesus, as a man, did not fit the qualifications of the Melchizedek order. It was only as he understood the Christ within that Jesus was *made* a high priest forever after the order of the Melchizedek.[51] The word *made* means a process or a transition. When he became enlightened to his Christ Identity, he immediately moved into another order. Religion has never taught anything of the Melchizedek order, yet it appears in the Scripture four more times than the words "born again". Why? Because you cannot see or understand the Melchizedek order until you first come to the realization that Christ dwells within you as you. This knowledge of your Christ consciousness, or Christ-Self, arms you against the religious teaching of separation. It frees you from the illusion of a God that we need to fear. This knowledge also creates within, a space from which the original New Testament Church operated. It is a space that calls forth spirit and follows its guidance without the egoic intention of man.

If Jesus, as a man, could not fit the qualifications of the Melchizedek order, then who could? What could these qualifications possibly be?

---

50 *Matthew 16:16*
51 *Hebrews 6:20*

Actually, they are simple: no mother or father, no beginning or ending of days, and no descent. Although Jesus was very spiritual, he had a mother and a father. He had a beginning and an ending of days, and he had a descent and nationality. He was born of the tribe of Judah and therefore was Hebrew in the flesh. Christ is the one with whom you can find no mother or father, no beginning or end. Christ is neither Jew nor Gentile, male nor female. It is the *Christ* Jesus, not Jesus Christ, who is after the order of Melchizedek. It is not by accident that sometimes the Scriptures say Jesus Christ and other times Christ Jesus. The arrangement of the names is a clue in the Bible. Most people know Jesus Christ. But there are also people who know Christ Jesus. Jesus Christ is the flesh or man revealing spirit. Christ Jesus is the spirit revealing the man.

The Bible tells us that Christ is *plural* and has many members, not just the one. [52] "He that is joined unto the Lord is one spirit."[53] Christ has united with your spirit. Your individual personality, which makes you unique from others, makes you an individual. You are the builder of your own individuality. Your ability of free will has built your personality. Once we get out of only knowing ourselves as personalities, we can get into the true essence of that which we are-- the substance of self, or spirit. As the extension of God, you are also spirit. Your essence is not flesh, thought or consciousness. Your essence *is* spirit. You are a spirit living in a physical body. You are spirit, for God is spirit. It is time to discover your deity self in a fleshly body. This is the reason that you are on earth. Pierre Teilhard de Chardin said, "We are not human beings having a spiritual experience. We are spiritual beings having a human experience." This is the essence of who we are as spiritual beings living in physical bodies. We are in an effort to experience humanity through the flesh and to rediscover our spiritual substance. As Jesus came into the recognition of his Christ, or of his indwelling spirit, he came into a union with the Father. The Father and the Christ became one. He could literally say that the Christ within him is also the Father. Jesus prayed that you would become one with Him (the Father) as he has done. In the same respect, God reminds us that we are one with Christ.

---
52 *I Corinthians 12:12*
53 *I Corinthians 6:17*

> "Know ye not that your bodies are the members of Christ? Shall I then take the members of Christ and make them members of an harlot? God forbid. What? Know ye not that he which is joined to an harlot is one body?"[54]

This passage is not referring to a woman as a prostitute out on the street! It is referring to the harlot *system*. God forbid that the body of Christ should lay with the harlot system. When that happens, the body becomes one with her. Do you remember lying with the harlot system of religion? You looked just like her. You dressed and spoke just like her. Everybody looked and talked alike. Verse 17 says, "He that is joined unto the Lord is one spirit." This is the key to understanding our own Christ element. We are not only *of* the creation but are *part of the deity that created*. We are Elohiym-- the term used when the Scriptures say, "God created." It may be a term that you are not familiar with because religion has not taught it; but the word Elohiym appears in the original script of the Old Testament over 2,500 times! "Elohiym" does not mean God in a singular form, but is a word like Christ, meaning many members. In the Hebrew, it says gods. This same word is used in Psalm 82 where it says, "Ye are gods (Elohiym), and all of you are children of the Most High." God takes out of Himself, Himself, and becomes individualized as Elohiym the Co-Creators. That is why Genesis says, "Let *us* make man." Religion has taught that the appearance of "us" refers to the trinity; but nowhere do the Scriptures limit Elohiym to the existence of only three deities. Ephesians says the *whole* family in heaven and earth has been given the name (I AM).

---

54   I Corinthians 6:15-16

AGREE WITH YOUR ADVERSARY

We spend an entire lifetime fighting battles with opposing forces. Perhaps the most difficult of Jesus' instructions to follow is "Agree with thine adversaries quickly… " But difficulty is only a result of lack of *understanding*. We hear many voices, which appear to be destructive forces, but as the consciousness is raised through understanding, it discovers that in reality, an adversary can only be destructive when it is *perceived* to be destructive. As we come to the inner knowledge of the "oneness of all forces", we see life, light, and love-- God, in all things.

Each individual is a spiritual creation with a definite purpose for being in the earth. The mission of each is different; therefore, the preparation for each is different. Our unwillingness to allow one another our experiences as tools for growth causes pain and division. True deliverance and understanding comes by truly being in the experience of each situation that we encounter. There is hope for all of humanity as we learn the simple, yet complex lesson that our adversaries are not what they appear to be. Our adversaries are instruments of spirit, clothed in many different forms, with the purpose of teaching humanity that God is in all.

> "Agree with thine adversary quickly, whiles thou are in
> the way with him, lest at any time the adversary deliver

thee to the judge, and the judge deliver thee to the officer, and thou be cast into prison." Matthew 5:25

The word, *agree* comes from the Greek word *eunoeo,* which means *to be well minded or reconciled.* It is a composite of two Greek words: *eu,* meaning *good or well done,* and *nous,* meaning *mind or understanding.*

The word *adversary* comes from two Greek words: *anti,* meaning *opposite or instead of,* and *dike,* meaning *justice, right or judgment.* To agree (be well minded) with your adversary (anti-judgment situation) means being able to look at a person or situation appearing to be against you with enlightened understanding. In other words, to *agree with your adversary* means to *have a good **understanding** of your adversary.* It is *not* to agree in judgment or words but to understand your adversary so you view the circumstance with a spiritual perspective; see it from a healthy perception and harmonize it to work for the highest good. This is agreeing.

"And all things are of God, who hath reconciled us unto Himself by Jesus Christ and hath given to us the ministry of reconciliation." II Corinthians 5:18

The word reconciliation comes from the Greek word *Katallasso,* meaning *adjustment, restoration to divine favor, to settle a difference.* Reconciliation is the Holy Spirit's capability to adjust the mind into a position to see the adversary as a potential opportunity for growth and development. It takes the perception of a situation, understands it to be a projection of the ego, and places it in the overall purpose of Spirit. The ultimate wisdom of the Holy Spirit, in the administration of reconciliation, is to perceive an adversary by *relinquishing all judgment.* A person who can "agree" is one who understands an anti-judgment situation and can settle any difference through adjusting and restoring all involved in divine favor with a healthy outlook.

We become weak in our outlook on life when we perceive a particular situation as being evil, when it actually contains the potential for good. We become weak in our outlook when we perceive the source to be Satan or an adversary, when in reality, it is God. Let's look at some examples of how this outlook on life is unhealthy:

> "And again the anger of the Lord was kindled against Israel, and He moved David against them to say, go number Israel." II Samuel 24:1

> "And Satan stood up against Israel and provoked David to number Israel." I Chronicles 21:1

Here we see two recordings of David being provoked to number Israel. One account expresses that he was provoked by Satan, while the other account expresses that he was provoked by God. On the surface, this is not a healthy translation. The word Satan, in the second account, comes from the Hebrew word that means adversary-- but is translated as "Satan"! The truth of these two seemingly opposing statements is that David's adversary was *God*. What is represented in these scriptures has nothing to do with the Satan that is presented to us by religion. God was the adversary that provoked David to number Israel. If you look at these two scriptures through the above concept of reconciliation, the differences that appear on the surface become clear through a healthy viewpoint. They are not against one another. In reality, they are saying the same thing. We find another example of this in Numbers 22:22:

> "And God's anger was kindled because he (Balaam) went and the angel of the Lord stood in the way for an adversary against him…"

Balaam's disobedience angered God; but in God's desire to rid Balaam from rebellion, an adversary was sent to stand in his way. This adversary, sent by God, literally saved Balaam's life.

Look again at the scriptural instructions "agree with your adversary quickly while you are in the way with him." The word *way* comes from the Greek word *hodos* meaning *progress, mode or means*. So many areas are adjusted and brought into alignment when we remember that we are the children of God. The journey begins in the moment of awakening, and the avenues of redemption begin to unfold. That which appears to be an adversary will often be the vehicle of salvation. Our adversaries, like Balaam's, can literally save our lives once we acknowledge that God is at the core of all things. A healthy mind comes from this attitude.

A person who has this healthy-mind can look at outer circumstances and see within them to find the truth of the matter. In this state of awareness, one controls the circumstances of life, instead of allowing the circumstances to control him or her. Growth and maturity brings the expertise needed to observe all circumstances through an intense sensitivity. By having a good understanding of anti-judgment situations, comes the discovery that only a wrong perception causes a situation to work negatively. This is the key to unlocking the chains of defeat and limitation.

> "Though the Lord give you the bread of adversity and the waters of affliction, yet shall thy teachers not be removed in a corner anymore, but thine eyes shall see thine teachers, and thine ears shall hear a word saying, this is the way, walk ye in it..." Isaiah 30:20,21

The bread of adversity and the waters of affliction are our teachers. A defensive attitude cannot help you develop a good understanding of anti-judgment situations. We cannot learn from the things that we encounter if anger, resentment, or fear controls us. Every situation in life contains a lesson for us to learn. Only through a true understanding of these lessons, and a lack of resistance when they are presented, can we be fulfilled. People continually wander through the wilderness of confusion repeating old reactionary patterns.

Focusing on a situation, and empowering it with negativity, causes this unhealthy attitude, or wrong perception. You should ask yourself the question, "Why am I encountering this situation?" Every condition must be evaluated by how it relates to others, only then can the encounter be understood. Rebellion, anger, insecurity, and fear may be hiding within. Like attracts like; and until there is a complete adjustment of all wrong attitudes, it is the wrong attitudes that will continue to recreate in your body and affairs. The bread of affliction becomes the adversary needed to bring these things to light. Once we recognize that spirit and truth are contained within the core of every situation, the adversity or problem becomes the teacher. This is when we hear "This is the way, walk ye in it!"

> "Not that I speak in respect of want, for I have learned in whatever state I am, therewith to be content."
> Philippians 4:11

This place of contentment can be discovered in the experience of all situations encountered. With the right perception, it becomes clear that all situations contain elements for tremendous growth and learning. This is agreeing with your adversary. "We know all things work together for good..."[55] yet at the same time, we cry out for God to deliver us from "all things". This double-minded attitude creates great instability because of lack of understanding. In the original text, this scripture reads "all things cooperate with each other." With this adjustment, it becomes clear that no matter what the situation, one can always find the "eye of the hurricane". The wind may blow around you-- but stand still and know that I AM!

A total lack of peace is the result of a mind that always looks for the rapture-- a way of "instant" escape. Before we can have deliverance out of a situation, we must be delivered *in* a situation. Daniel was not delivered *out* of the lion's den until he was first delivered while *in* the lion's den. He did not come out of the lion's den to be delivered - he came out already delivered! The three Hebrew children did not come out of the fire to be delivered-- they were delivered while they were yet in the fire. It is the chains, the limitations, which are burned in the fire, when we stop fighting and start agreeing with our adversaries.

The consuming fire of God's love creates a fiery furnace for us IF that is what we need to be free of our limitations. The fire itself is sometimes nothing more than the answer to a prayer. This is why situations repeat themselves; people pray for deliverance while wandering around the same cycles of confusion thinking their prayers are not being answered. Until there is understanding of the situation, true deliverance cannot occur.

Jesus is the classic example of a miracle worker because He shifted His perception to the essential self-- the Christ. He was able to view His perceptions, formed by the society and religion of His day, as His adversaries. When He faced the adversary in the wilderness, He knew it was not an entity outside of Himself. There was nothing outside of

---

55 *Romans 8:28*

Himself that could have been a temptation. The devil was not a little pitchfork carrying, red-horned monster out to get Jesus! A fallen angel would have presented Jesus no problem. His temptation had to be closer to home, something within Himself, for He was "in all points tempted as we are, yet without sin".[56] His adversary was His mind tempting Him to use His deity out of alignment with the will of God.

Once we tap into the kingdoms' power and authority, we will face the same temptations as Jesus. As you realize you have the creative power of life or death, you will be tempted to use this power out of alignment with God's purpose. We must learn now, through the small things, to agree with and to understand, our adversaries. Then we will be qualified to rise above the greatest temptation of all, the perception of the egoic mind. By agreeing, you attain a good understanding of all anti-judgment situations.

> "Submit yourselves to God, resist the devil and he will flee from you." James 4:7

Submission to God comes through inner recognition that the essence of Spirit is contained within the heart of all things. The word devil is the Greek word *diabolos* meaning *accuser or adversary*. To resist the devil, your adversary, is reverse psychology. It is not a matter of acknowledging or giving power, it is understanding that each perception has caused a certain condition. Anything that appears destructive and brings fear is an illusion, a shadow-- unreality that cannot harm you. The minute you understand this, you agree with your adversary. You agree with your circumstance and you become content with whatever you are experiencing. Each situation we encounter can be transmuted from problems that have caused weakness to stepping stones that produce great strength.

---

56 *Hebrews 4:15*

How to Stay Out of Prison

What happens when you do not agree with your adversaries? Two things: first, you go before the judge, who sends you to the officer, who sends you to prison. What you must understand is that you are all of these: the judge, the officer and the prison! No one judges you, but yourself! The awakened child of God will judge the world and angels.[57] The way of judgment is learned through experiences. Only you can pass a judgment and cast yourself into prison. By not having a healthy outlook, a mind that has a good understanding of the adversary, YOU start thinking that you have done something wrong. YOU bring yourself before the judge. YOU find yourself guilty. YOU pass the sentence and YOU execute that sentence by casting yourself into prison.

The word *judge*, in our beginning scriptures, comes from the Greek word *krites* meaning *to decide mentally, to think, go to law*. What is the one thing that causes you to think you are guilty? Wrong perceptions, caused by a belief in separation, holds you under the law of sin and death. This law brings the knowledge of sin, or that which forever points out that humanity has "missed the mark". YOU make a mental decision that YOU are guilty, based on wrong perceptions.

The word prison is from the Greek word *phulake* meaning *guarding, the act, person, place, or condition, a cage or hold*. It comes from the base word *phulasse*, meaning *the idea of isolation, to watch, prevent escape*. Once you decide that you are guilty, you are held captive to that which isolates you from reality and holds you in mental deception. You begin to put up your guard against people and conditions and your mind begins to play tricks on you, making you believe you are a victim. All thoughts that are habitually qualified by your beliefs will eventually manifest as the outer conditions of your life.

After Judas betrayed Jesus, he came to himself and repented of what he had done; the law said "an eye for an eye". Judas was under this law and knew nothing of grace, therefore he judged himself guilty and worthy of death. "The wages of sin is death" If you live by that law, you die by that law. What could Judas do but take his own life? It was not that he committed suicide; he carried out his own death sentence. He

---

57   *I Corinthian 6:1-3*

judged himself guilty, pronounced the sentence of death and became his own executioner.

When we turn from grace to law, we act in the same way that Judas did when he took his own life. We bring harm upon others and ourselves with our judgment. We have thrown the book at others and ourselves many, many times and God has had nothing to do with it! How can we stay out of our own prison? By having a good understanding of all situations, knowing they are not as they appear to be on the surface.

Inner wisdom directs us to relinquish all judgment and judge nothing. No one could know all of the facts pertaining to a situation or the persons involved. It becomes difficult for the awakened child of God to refrain from judgment. By relinquishing judgment, the true self can see all things from the aspect of total love.

It is time to review all anti-judgment situations that we think of as unfair or undeserving. A shift in perception opens an entirely different perspective. When we turn within, we awaken to the reality that God has never judged us guilty. The ego has brought the accusation, not God. Misperception began with a belief in separation, and by the ego's attempt to perceive someone or something as it thinks it should be, rather than as it is. You are not your outer self. You are spirit, your essential self. Turn within and see the real you. You will discover that you are not guilty of the illusions of false perceptions. God sees no one as guilty. When you see the real you, your spirit in alignment with God spirit, you will find that all those things which you allowed to bring great condemnation, in reality, do not even exist. You are not those outward actions. Those actions are only the projection of the ego in the outer world. The days of misconceptions can end when you allow the Holy Spirit to adjust your thoughts, ending all appearances of guilt and pain.

The adversaries of life will not end until we turn our focus within. False perceptions give illusions the appearance of life. We impart life to a "dead" situation by giving it a name, a nature. Consider this example: suppose someone who knows nothing of dogs is taught that dogs are poisonous and deadly. Because people react to situations by the way they perceive them to be, this person would probably be terrified of dogs. People, places, and things have no power within themselves; we give them power through recognition.

Religion has done this same thing with its false perception and projection of the devil. It has given something power that is not a reality, by calling it real. It calls illusion, reality; people believe in the illusion, empower it and react to it. But, in true reality, illusions only have power when they become real in a person's mind. Illusions are nothing more than a shadow created by an image that comes between God and us. Many times, out of fear, people react to certain conditions, later learning that the conditions were not as they appeared to be. It was not the person or thing, but what was going on in the person's mind that caused the reaction. Whatever the ego perceives a thing to be is what gives it power. The same is true with the outer self. Jesus came into the earth realm and took upon Himself flesh and blood that He might destroy (render inactive[58]) the illusion of the power of death, the devil (or the adversary.[59])

> *Now* is the judgment of this world: *now* shall the prince of this world be cast out. (St John 12:31)

The *now* was 2000 years ago during Jesus' time. Why do we continue to fight something that has already been rendered inactive? Once you see truth, the understanding of the illusion will set you free. An illusion has no substance or power. All that an illusion has is the *appearance* of power.

How can something that is not real hurt you? The mind has great power and ability to create whatever it gives thought to, because the emotions cause the imagination to run wild. The ego is the maker of illusions. When you know the truth of the matter, that it is from vain imagination, the understanding of this brings enlightenment to the mind. Standing in agreement with truth causes the struggles and labors of the mind to end. Much of the world's problems stem from the overworked imagination. It is what causes wars and rumors of war. Our problems appear real because we imagine something that is not real and magnify it totally out of proportion. The ego is our only enemy, and yet it is the last enemy with which we choose to deal. Only the egoic mind retains the power of death. The Scripture tells us death is the last enemy to be destroyed. How does death have power? Through

---

58 from the Greek word: katargeo
59 *Hebrews 2:14*

the perception of the mind! Therefore, the egoic (carnal) mind is the last enemy.

We have been given the ministry of reconciliation. It is time to settle all differences and to start within. As all situations of life are viewed from a consciousness that has been renewed by truth, no longer perceiving adversaries as evil, we will be able to declare the end from the beginning. There is much truth waiting to be revealed that has never been tapped. This truth cannot come until we learn to settle all differences through the eyes of God. We must understand all antijudgment situations and allow them to work their purpose.

As we observe all things in their finished state, we attract that which we need to attain our goal and to fulfill our destiny. There is a time for cursing and a time for blessing. Sometimes you need an enemy to tell you the truth. Friends can be our worst enemies because, out of love, they are afraid the truth might hurt us and/or destroy the friendship. Constructive criticism is healthy, even if it comes through the voice of an adversary. Truth sets us free, no matter what it is or from whom it comes.

To be content in all situations is to find your true state of being, not being affected by outer conditions, but controlled from inner conditions. We have tried to find our identity or true essence in other people, places, and things, but it must come from *within*. As we live, move and have our being through the reality of the indwelling Christ, people, places, and things will not dictate our reality. Our inner reality will dictate all of our life's conditions. In this state of being, nothing else will matter. *Agree with your adversary.* Stop fighting and see your adversary as the child of God. See the image of God in all things, and you will find a peace and joy that surpasses all human understanding. You will *become* a testimony rather than *have* a testimony! People will ask, "What makes you different? How is it that you have joy and peace in the midst of adverse situations?" Doors will swing open and you will be able to introduce "Christ in you," the real Christ. You will have total dominion to speak words of spirit and life to the earth, and the earth will yield its fruit.

Agree with your adversary quickly, lest you go before the judge and the officer, and be cast into prison. There is no reason to walk into prison any longer. You are not being called into prison! Joseph went to prison, but he chose to agree with his adversary rather than fight the situation. Later, his adversary became that which fed his family in times of famine. While yet in prison, he came to know who he was, rose to a high place and became a ruler over the land. An adversary sometimes gives to you what you minister to creation. Your experiences become strength, compassion, and insight to enable you to relinquish all judgment. Eventually, there will be gods who only know and see God in all things! The ability to recognize God in every situation will bring forth a light that dispels everything that is not of a redeemable nature.

Love Thy Enemy

Our perceptions must shift so that we see all adversaries as situations formed by wrong attitudes. For all of those times when we have felt "trapped" in a lesser quality of life, we can now reflect upon those times and consider them anew: all experiences have been and *are* for our continued growth. To take the opportunity to awaken at the earth level is to recognize God in all things. It is to recognize each experience as another stepping-stone rather than a stumbling block.

When we have reached a place of truly being ready for growth, each experience can become another page in the book of life, simply by bringing to life a willingness to grow and meet the true face of God. It is said, "When the student is ready, the teacher will come". It is possible that when you are ready, your teacher will be presented to you as an adversary. In this respect, we must learn to agree quickly with our adversaries in all situations. The Scriptures teach us that patience is a godly virtue, which must be allowed to work a perfect work, that we may be perfect, entire and wanting nothing. Through faith and patience we inherit the promise. "Ye have need of patience that after ye have done the will of God, ye might receive the promise."[60] Each individual must learn the lesson of patience as we walk through humanity. Remember

---

60   *Hebrews 10:36*

that we are all walking through humanity *together*. We are not alone. Recognize your adversary through the eyes of love - the eyes of God. And in so doing, you recognize your spirit, your family, and your teachers.

Agree with your adversary. Take time to discern every person, place, and situation you encounter that you may come to a full and complete understanding of all situations. Shifting your perception will cause all illusions of pain, guilt, and heartache to be transmuted into peace, joy, and love. You will never again allow yourself to be the prisoner of a situation. You will control all emotions that govern your own life and be able to give peace to all whose paths you cross. Adversaries become friends and you fulfill the words of Jesus when you relinquish all judgment and "love (*understand*) your enemies".

Releasing Spirits

It is in essence, (that which makes something what it is), that there are no "evil spirits." But there are spirits with evil attitudes or dispositions.

Knowledge has increased dramatically over the last decade bringing tremendous change to lifestyles, education, and research. Modern technology has produced an age of computers, push button conveniences, and expansion into outer space. The Scriptures foretold of a time when the knowledge of the Lord would cover the earth as the waters cover the sea[61]. The stage has been set for a renewing in the hearts of all mankind to a youthful vitality that is restoring enthusiasm, confidence, and creativity.

We live in a country of great magnitude at one level, yet at another level we see unbelievable spiritual ignorance and darkness. Man's ability to perceive truth has taken a ninety degree turn, and truth is finding an avenue of expression in the hearts and minds of untold numbers of people who are searching for answers to personal problems; domestic as well as foreign. No longer will the lies that have held the world in ignorance be allowed full sway over the minds of mankind.

---

61   Habakkuk 2:14

David Hulse, D.D.

There has always been those in the earth who have broken out of the dogma of narrow minded thinking imposed by society, culture, and religion. They have been behind the scenes, unknown by the majority. The escalation of natural knowledge is evidence that those behind the scenes have experienced extraordinary breakthroughs in spiritual knowledge and understanding. The principles that are being uncovered will be given to the multitudes of humanity. Spiritual education will increase with the same magnitude that has been seen in the natural. Just as outer space has been explored, so shall inner space be explored.

The principles presented in this article totally challenge the majority of religious thought on the subject of untimely deaths, such as suicide and accidents, and the mysterious phenomena that has been called every thing from demon possession to insanity. This subject is not presented as an in depth study, but as thoughts to quicken the mind to a remembrance of the truth once known. Creation must be touched at all levels, not in words of man's wisdom, but in a power and demonstration that will carry with it answers for peace and harmony. Wisdom, knowledge, and understanding contain the stability that will bring full restoration to the universe.

Many times the Scripture is quoted: "Jesus Christ the same yesterday, today, and forever.[62]" How often we hear: "If it was good enough for Grandma, it's good enough for me." That is ignorance! God never changes, but man's understanding and comprehension of God does. The elements to produce electricity did not originate with Thomas Edison. The knowledge and understanding to harness and produce electricity made its appearance in the earth through a man who gave his life to producing the manifestation of a principle, which he uncovered. The elements capable of producing electricity had always been, but only through tapping into the knowledge and understanding of the principles was it brought to manifestation.

The truth man is discovering today was once known and understood, but it is only perceived and accepted by those who dare to step outside the boundaries of narrow minded thinking. One must dare to pursue thoughts and principles which will challenge the ignorance of chasing rainbows and fighting shadows. As you read this chapter, allow your mind to be freed from all limitations. Erase all lines that have been drawn, for a plan of salvation is unfolding which knows no boundaries.

---

62 Hebrews 13:8

Reconciliation

It is easy to believe that all men walking upon the face of the earth, in physical bodies can be reconciled to God, but what about those who have left the physical realm, yet needing a word and the ministry of reconciliation?

> "For I would not, brethren, that ye should be ignorant of this mystery: that blindness in part is happened to Israel, until the fullness of the Gentiles be come in. And so ALL ISRAEL SHALL BE SAVED...So I ask, have they stumbled so as to fall to their utter spiritual ruin, irretrievably? BY NO MEANS! But through their false step and transgressions salvation has come to the Gentiles, so as to arouse Israel to see and feel what they forfeited and so to make them jealous. Now, if their stumbling, their lapse, their transgression has so enriched the world, think what an enrichment and greater advantage their FULL REINSTATEMENT" (Rom.11:25 KJV, Rom. 11:12 Amp. Trans.)[63]

We read in this passage of Scripture, that due to blindness, Israel was led to transgression. A most remarkable question is asked: Has their stumbling caused them to fall to utter spiritual ruin? The answer, by no means! It goes on to speak of a FULL REINSTATEMENT. The ministry of reconciliation goes far beyond those walking upon the face of the earth in physical bodies. There are many in a place of spiritual ruin in the realm of spirit who are waiting for a ministry of love and mercy that will bring full reinstatement.

> "And having made peace through the blood of his cross, by him to reconcile ALL THINGS unto himself; by him I say, whether they be things in heaven, or things in earth" (Col. 1:20).

---

63 Please read from Rom. 11:8-26

Heaven has been so presented as a place of total perfection that few have dared to consider the possibility that anything in heaven could ever have need of reconciliation. Heaven speaks of the realm of spirit, that which is beyond form or matter. Heaven is the abode of God or eternity. In the heavens, the realm of spirit, eternity, there are many different levels or realms. All spirits go back to God from whence they came (Ec. 12:7). It matters not if the spirit is enlightened or not. All spirits return to the heavens or the abode of God. In this place, they are reserved until an appointed time when the heavens shall receive Jesus the Christ and members of His body. At the time of the restitution of all things that has been spoken by the mouth of the Holy prophets, full reinstatement will be given. (Acts 3:19,20).

> "And all things are of God, who hath reconciled us unto Himself by Jesus Christ, and hath given to us the ministry of reconciliation; to wit, that God was in Christ, reconciling the world unto Himself, not imputing their trespasses unto them; and hath committed unto US the word of reconciliation" (IICor. 5:18,19).

In this Scripture, we see two different levels of reconciliation; the "ministry" and the "word" of reconciliation. The word reconciliation means: "adjustment, restoration to divine favor, to settle a difference, to restore harmony." True reconciliation is understanding and wisdom to take any person or situation that appears to be either positive or negative, put it in its proper place, and know where it fits in the overall purpose of spiritual destiny.

First, let's consider the "**WORD**" of reconciliation. "Word" in the original text is logos; "a thought, topic, doctrine, mental faculty, divine expression." Tremendous revelation has been given on the topic of reconciliation by a divine expression. Many books have been written, and messages given concerning the truth that all men are Spirit, made in the image and likeness of God. That "word" was committed, meaning "given for consideration and report." This is exactly what has taken place; a message has been presented and considered. This in itself is beautiful, for the principles of any topic must first be revealed. However, as so often is the case, truth can be lost in knowledge with no power to produce the effect.

Next, let's consider the "**ministry** of reconciliation." The word "ministry" means "attendance, to look after, take charge, be present with, apply mind, pay. "A true ministry is a commission bestowed by formal action, put into possession, and delivered by bodily action. The ministry of reconciliation goes far beyond knowledge. It will cause a feeling and knowing of oneness with all of creation. In other words, the principles of the knowledge acquired begin to be applied by unction of the Spirit. The needs of others become foremost in thought and action. As this ministry unfolds, bodily action or true involvement begins. It's easy to present and consider a word, which has been revealed by a Divine Expression, but it must go beyond mere words and come into a living expression.

> "I exhort therefore, that, first of all, supplications, prayers, intercessions, and giving of thanks, be made for ALL MEN... For this is good and acceptable in the sight of God our Savior; who will have ALL MEN TO BE SAVED AND COME TO THE KNOWLEDGE OF TRUTH" (I Tim. 2:1,3,4).

The word "will" means "determined." God has determined that ALL MEN shall be saved. As the ministry of reconciliation is entered, a determination unfolds to see all people and situations harmonized. Obedience to the instructions of Spirit will lead into levels of ministry that were never considered to be a part of reconciling all things back to God. At this point, the boundaries are broken.

> "For we wrestle not against flesh and blood, but against principalities, against powers, against the rulers of the darkness of this world, against spiritual wickedness in HIGH (heavenly) places..."(Eph. 6:12).

> "We according to his promise look for new heavens and a new earth, wherein dwelleth righteousness" (II Pet. 3:13).

The word "high" speaks of heavenly or celestial. This is speaking of spiritual wickedness in heavenly places, or in the realm beyond form and matter. Peter speaks of the heavens passing away with a great noise and being on fire, symbolic of cleansing. The realm of the heavens is as the realm of the earth, only the occupants create wickedness. If there were not a need for those in the heavens or the realm of spirit to be ministered to and brought to restoration, the Scripture would not speak of looking for a NEW heaven where righteousness would dwell. There is a great need for all limitations and wrong perceptions to be transcended, both in heaven as well as the earth. A consciousness must be penetrated which does not see any boundaries between heaven and earth to bring salvation to both realms.

Reconciliation does not operate within the boundaries of preconceived ideas and perceptions. It hears the cry of all men, whether in the body or out of the body, to be recognized as the offspring of God. It does not judge by appearance and has a profound ability, through wisdom and understanding, to restore men back to their original estate.

Releasing Spirits

We have dealt with the fact that all men are made in the image and likeness of God, which is Spirit. All Spirit returns to God from whence it came and all things, whether in heaven or in earth will be reconciled back unto God. There has been much controversy over the validity of claims that people can be possessed by the devil. We do not deny the fact that many people have been involved in horrible experiences that seem to be connected to the realm of "devils and evil." I cannot say often enough, however, truth will make men free. I now want to look at some Scriptures that show a definite difference between devils and spirits.

> "And it came to pass afterward, that he went throughout every city and village, preaching and showing the glad

tidings of the kingdom of God: And the twelve went with him, and certain women, which had been healed of evil spirits and infirmities, Mary called Magdalene, out of whom was cast seven devils and Joanna the wife of Chuza, Herod's steward, and many others, which ministered unto him of their substance" (Luke 8: 1-3).

In this Scripture we see a distinction made between "casting out devils" and "healing one with evil spirits." Jesus gave His disciples' power to cast out both devils and heal those with evil spirits. It has been assumed that casting out devils and evil spirits was the same thing. A lot of things, however, have been assumed that are far from truth.

The word spirits in the original text is pneuma meaning "the rational soul, mental disposition, Divine God, Christ Spirit, and Holy Spirit." God is Spirit (John 4:24) and all spirits came out of God and return to God (Ec. 12:7). There are no stipulations on this statement, nor does it matter the condition of the one who has housed the spirit while in the earth realm. A spirit can be enlightened or unenlightened. Spirit is a word expressing the mind of the spirit, where all thoughts, actions and experiences are recorded. Every time the word spirit is used in the New Testament (except twice when the disciples saw Jesus walking on the water and thought he was a "ghost," rendered "spirit" in the N.T.), it is pneuma. It matters not if it refers to the Holy Spirit, or to an evil or unclean spirit. The substance that all men have been made of is spirit. It has been called many things: the human spirit, a bad spirit, a good spirit, an unclean spirit, and an evil spirit. But ALL spirit is God substance.

It is in essence (that which makes something what it is), that there are no "evil spirits." But there are spirits with evil attitudes or dispositions. There is only ONE universal spirit -- GOD. God created man in His image and His likeness; which is Spirit. Everything came out of God and by Him all things consist (Col. 1:16, 17). Everything that exists has to be spirit in essence. We must go beyond the consciousness of duality! What is referred to as an" evil spirit" is in reality an evil or distorted attitude which can create all kinds of external manifestations, but only because of the attitude. It is not the spirit that is evil, but the manifestation. Thoughts, feelings, emotions, desires, etc. are projected through a mind that is not in alignment with truth. As the purity of Spirit flows through a distorted mind, it too will project an evil image or feeling.

Let's use an example: A projector can only project the contents of the film that is run through the light. If you take a film of beautiful imagery and run it through a projector, it produces the effect of that which is pleasant. If through the same projector and the same light you ran a film of something distorted and wicked, it would produce the effect of that which is unpleasant. Images on film, either pleasant or unpleasant, can be run through the same projector and light, but it will be the contents of the film, not the projector that makes the difference. An evil spirit is only a projection of evil running through a mind that is distorted and looking at life backwards. As mentioned in a earlier chapter, the word e-v-i-l is l-i-v-e spelled backward. There are no evil spirits, only the appearance of evil running through the ego or carnal mind, projecting itself as evil.

The duality of good and evil is only in the mind, i.e. the way one thinks and perceives. The spirit is not conscious of the duality of good or evil. The separation begins in the mind, or the consciousness the spirit runs through. When the mind or the eye becomes single, the projection will always be single. The unity of true Spirit, or God consciousness always provides the mind with the availability to project only the image of life, void of all separation.

The words "evil" and "unclean" mean, "foul, to clog or obstruct with a foreign substance which brings dishonor and disrespect." When the Scripture speaks of an evil spirit, it is referring to a spirit that has lived in a physical body and left the physical realm in an evil or unclean consciousness. External, material, fleshly problems, which are a foreign substance to spirit, clog and obstruct the knowledge of true spirit substance. A spirit can leave the physical realm unenlightened or unregenerated because it did not come to the knowledge and understanding that all men are made in the image and likeness of God. All spirits have the right through the atonement (at-one-ment) of the blood, to go back to God. They lost their body and reward and no longer have an earthly place, but their hope is not destroyed. Paul spoke of the destruction of the flesh, that the spirit might be saved in the day of the Lord (I Cor. 5:5). Upon leaving the physical body, the spirit goes to a place of correction. (I Cor. 3:11-16).

The word "devil" in the original text is *daimon* meaning a supernatural spirit of a bad nature, *ademonic* being or a deity. Remember, Jesus destroyed the works of the devil which rendered him inactive.[64] In the perceptions of many people, the devil has become a separate entity. Since the resurrection, the "devil" has seemingly had strength because religion has taught men to recognize him. They have also taught that he has great power. There is no devil or demon that has any power over man, except the power that is rendered active by a mental belief. By this mental belief, one literally creates the power believed in and makes it active in his world.

Jesus spoke of signs that followed those who believe. One of these signs was "casting out devils" (Mark 16:17). The word "cast" means "to evict from property." By the name or nature of Christ, devils have no claim or right to man as their property. Thus the commission was to "cast devils" out of man's consciousness by teaching them the power of knowing the Truth. As the belief in the power of the devil is replaced with the belief in the power of the indwelling Christ, man's consciousness is freed from the duality of good and evil, and of the duality of God and Satan. By simple faith in the power of enlightenment, man can be free from all power of any devil, or any form of evil consciousness.

In the scriptures of Matthew 10:1 & Mark 3:13,14, we see three different realms of ministry which the twelve disciples were involved in: casting out devils, dealing with unclean or evil spirits and healing the sick. In the book of Acts we find a record of evil or unclean spirits, *not devils* being dealt with. There is no record of casting out devils after the time of Jesus. We must remember, there is a difference in devils and evil spirits. Therefore, let us understand what the Scripture is truly saying, for only in rightly dividing the word can we bring true deliverance.

> "But the manifestation of the Spirit is given to every man to profit with all. For to one is given by the Spirit the word of wisdom; to another the word of knowledge by the same Spirit, to another faith by the same Spirit; to another the gifts of healing by the same Spirit; to

---

64 Heb. 2:14

> another the working of miracles; to another prophecy, to another discerning of spirits..." (I Cor. 12:7-10)

The word "discerning" means, "to separate thoroughly." There is a great need for the discerning of spirits, not the discerning of devils. This is a manifestation of the Spirit which needs to be exercised and brought to maturity. To separate thoroughly is to know the difference in the manifestation of the carnal mind that projects an evil, or unclean spirit.

With this foundation laid, I now want to share a word spoken to me as I was on my way to a meeting in 1983 when I was impressed with these words, "I want you to release the spirit of someone who has committed suicide. His family and friend's beliefs are holding him captive and his spirit needs to be released. I need one who is an open channel to release him from being earth bound." After these words were spoken, the spirit world was opened to me in a way I had never comprehended, nor considered.

In Psalms 102:20 we read that each man has an appointment with death. Only as one comes to a God consciousness and begins to be filled with the fullness of God can he be released from his appointment with death. If a person leaves the physical realm before his appointed time, such as suicide, or an untimely death, he can become an earth bound spirit and not be allowed, at that time, to enter into the dimension of the spirit world. Grief of family and friends over a departed loved one can also hold a spirit captive. Whatever is recorded in the mind of the spirit, the feelings and desires, remains with that spirit after it leaves the physical body. A person who had a problem with drugs, alcohol or any uncontrollable habit, has the same desires and needs but, cannot find fulfillment because he no longer has a physical body.

Earthbound spirits become angry and distorted. Eventually they begin to look for a body through which they can fulfill their needs. They find and enter people who are despondent, depressed, and in hopeless situations, without the will to live. They can walk right into a body and take control. This accounts for some extreme cases of schizophrenia and sudden personality changes. Scripture tells us "what is bound in earth is bound in heaven." "Heaven" being the dimension outside of the physical realm. Where the tree falls so shall it lie. (Ec.

11:3) When a person leaves the physical realm bound by any conditions that have not been balanced in the *life stream* (soul), one will take that unfinished business with him/her out of the body. Here one has an option of going back into the earth realm to finish out the balancing of ones actions and choices, or to do it out of the body (which is a much slower process).

An unclean or evil spirit is not limited to suicide cases alone. Those who are extremely rebellious and live corrupted lives can also become earthbound spirits. Some are simply undeveloped souls. This is where the "discerning of souls" is desperately needed. As we realize that we wrestle not with flesh and blood, nor with a devil, but sometimes with a soul that is earthbound, we will find true and lasting deliverance come to many situations that have been unaffected by religious rhetoric and religious rituals.

A ministry is being prepared for the releasing of these spirits. When an earthbound spirit takes possession of a body, in reality, he is crying out for deliverance. It is time to stop BINDING and start RELEASING these spirits. Every time one is cast out bound, he goes immediately in search of another body.

> "When the unclean spirit is gone out of a man, he walketh through dry places, seeking rest and find thee none. Then he saith, I will return into my house from whence I came out..." (Matt. 12:43,44).

To walk through dry places refers to a place void of the presence of God. The word rest is re-creation meaning "to create anew, restore, refresh." When these souls are bound and cast out, they seek to be restored. Until they are released, they cannot find their place of rest and restoration. The minute they are loosed, they can go into the God dimension and find their place of correction, which will bring renewal and restoration. As these spirits enter a body, they are crying out, "Loose me!" Stop binding and casting them into outer darkness. Release them and send them into the light or fire of God! Only in this dimension can they find re-creation.

There have been greater problems created by the wrong kind of deliverance than if it had been left totally alone. Every time you bind and cast a soul out, you are the one prolonging the deliverance of that spirit and causing the next person he enters to become a victim. Religious rhetoric has been parroted long enough! It is past time for a true ministry of deliverance! These spirits want to be released, but when attacked in the name of Jesus, they fight back and resist because they know they are not free to go into the Spirit dimension. They know they will only have to find another body to occupy. Deliverance preachers have been binding and casting out spirits for years. This is why the cycle continually repeats itself. The blind has led the blind and the whole world has fallen into a pit of ignorance from lack of knowledge and understanding.

> "For this cause was the gospel preached ALSO to them that are dead, that they might be judged as men in the flesh, but live according to God in the spirit" (IPet. 4:6).

> "For Christ also hath once suffered for sins, the just for the unjust, that he might bring us to God, being put to death in the flesh, but quickened in the spirit: By which also he preached to the spirits in prison" (I Pet. 3:18, 19).

In these scriptures, we read that Jesus preached the gospel to those who were dead, to spirits in prison. The works that He did, we shall do also. He is the Head of His body and wherever the Head goes, the body follows. Earthbound spirits must be released! This is a part of the ministry of reconciliation. This realm of ministry goes far beyond appearance and religious tactics. To bring reconciliation to all things, we must look past all manifestations of flesh and hear the cries of creation. It matters not the intensity of the situation. The ministry of reconciling all things back to God begins with an attitude that can look at all people and say, "Father forgive them for they know not what they do." God needs a body in which to appear. He cannot use someone with a traditional consciousness that sees only heaven-hell, black-white, right-wrong and is ready to push everyone into hell. He needs the availability of a person who knows the love and mercy of the Most High. He needs a person who understands that man was made subject to vanity, not willingly, but by reason of hope in God's power to redeem all things (Rom. 8:20,21).

We have received testimonies from people who were unable to receive deliverance through the ritual of "binding" and casting out devils. As spirits are released, tremendous things begin to happen. The reality and depth of truth holds immense power for liberation. Truth is not just a revelation. It is the awakened Sons of God actually fulfilling their function and becoming God's instruments in the earth, daring to step beyond all boundaries. Creation groans to be released -- not only the creation in physical bodies, but creation in all dimensions. Authority and wisdom to understand and minister love and forgiveness to unclean, or evil spirits opens up new avenues of possibilities. As this ministry develops, answers will come to situations that have seemed hopeless in the past.

> "Babylon the great is fallen, and is become the habitation of devils, and the hold of every foul (unclean) spirit... Come out of her, my people, that ye be not partakers of her sins, and that ye receive not of her plagues" (Rev. 18:2,4).

The words, "habitation" and "hold" speak of a place of imprisonment. Babylon, the systems of this world, has given devils a dwelling place. Unclean spirits have been retained in prison because man has not understood the great need to release them into the mercy and righteous of God. The cry goes forth, "Come out of her, My people! Come out of the old ways of thinking." Those who choose to remain in the ignorance and darkness of perceiving everything that is wrong as devils needing to be bound and cast into outer darkness will partake of the sin of that system. Whatsoever is not of faith is sin, therefore, sin is unbelief in God's ability to bring full and total reinstatement to all. Unbelief is the only sin there is and the wages of sin is death. Again, come out from among those who deny the power of God to reconcile all that is in the heavens and the earth. The covenant of death can be broken in the consciousness of the one who dares to believe that God will wipe all tears from the eyes of His creation.

"There shall be no more death, neither sorrow, nor crying, neither shall there be any more pain: for the former things are passed away." (Rev. 21:4)

There is a place no vulture's eye has seen. (Job 28:7) Woe be to the inhabitants of the realms of an earthly consciousness, for the devil inhabits that place, given power by the mind of man. Rejoice, ye heavens, you who allow your minds to be elevated past the realm of forever binding and casting devils or evil spirits into outer darkness. Blessed are the merciful for they shall obtain mercy! You are the ones God has chosen and predestined to go beyond the veil of time and eternity and bring reconciliation to both worlds. As you release, you shall be released. As you minister the love, mercy, and grace of the Most High, you shall receive the same love, mercy, and grace which will bring transformation to your world.

The Other Side Of The Coin

I want to end this chapter by looking at the other side of the coin. For every negative, there is a positive. Just as unclean or evil spirits can enter man, so can the spirits of just men. The Old Testament saints, the cloud of witnesses (Heb. 11 &12), are finding a platform and a place of expression in you. David said, "I was glad when they said unto me, let us go into the house of the Lord" (Ps.122:1). You are that house of the Lord, for they without you cannot be made perfect (Heb. 11:40). Those Patriarchs that no longer have a physical body have much to say. Part of their perfection lies in being able to express to those yet in the earth realm. Not only do they need a body to speak through, but they are gathered at any meeting where a true Expression of the Christ is coming forth that they might hear the word reserved for this day.

The word that is now being revealed has been reserved for the end of the age of grace and is for the purpose of bringing in the age of righteousness. A word is being spoken that will turn each man to the Christ within his own being, taking the eyes off the preacher. As we are caught up to realms past a fleshly consciousness, we will see the very atoms of the body take on dramatic change. It was not the fetus of John the Baptist that leaped in the womb of Elizabeth, but the adult spirit of Elijah. Again, in this day, the very host of heaven is finding a body and an expression. We must be yielded vessels, for God will bring completion of His plan for the ages through those who are open and sensitive to areas never before considered.

It matters not if spirits are those of just men or unclean spirits -- this is the day of salvation for ALL! The full salvation for those in the spirit world will come through the ministry of reconciliation by the awakened Christ who is now walking in the earth. The Word has again become flesh and Saviors are appearing. The earth and the heavens will be cleansed and restored as the spirits of all time and eternity are released.

As I said in the beginning of this chapter, these things have been presented to stir up your pure mind. For thousands of years, man has attempted to find answers to certain situations that have seemed hopeless. Truth will bring answers and reality. Effort without lasting results can be a thing of the past. He that is joined to God's Spirit is made ONE spirit. All things were created by the word of God. In Him all things have their beginning and end. Everything started in God and everything will end in God. God created man in His image and likeness, which is spirit. In His ultimate plan, all spirits shall be restored to their first estate. ALL SHALL BE REINSTATED! This full reinstatement will be ministered to the entire universe. Stand and be God's availability in both the earth and in the heavens. Hasten this great day of the Lord! Declare the end from the beginning by calling those things which be not as though they were. "Behold the Lord's hand is not shortened, that it cannot save[65]... The Lord will cause righteousness and praise to spring forth before ALL NATIONS.[66]" This is your calling! This is your destiny!

---

65   Isaiah 59:1
66   Isaiah 61:11

The Point Of Return

The Great Returning

"In returning and rest, shall ye be saved." Isa 30:15

The invisible things of God are clearly seen and understood by the things that are made. (Rom: 1:20) We are able to understand the laws and principals of spirit by understanding the laws and principals of nature. The body was formed from the dust of the ground, and the dust returns to the ground as it was. Spirit returns to God who gave it. (Ecc. 12:7) In this lies the principal contained in the reconciliation of all men. All things return from whence they came. There is a law or principal of circularity which governs all realms in both heaven and earth.

> "The sun also riseth, and the sun goeth down, and hasteth to his place where he arose. The wind goeth toward the south, and turneth about unto the north; it whirleth about continually, and the wind returneth again according to his circuits. All rivers run into the sea; yet the sea is not full; unto the place from whence the rivers came thither they return again... The thing that hath been done, it is that which shall be; and that which is done is that which shall be done: and there is no new thing under the sun." (Ecc. 1:5-7, 9)

In this scripture we clearly see the principal of the law of circularity. Let's take a close look at this principal by using a circle as the symbol of God who has no beginning or end, but is Alpha and Omega, the beginning and end. If we saw God as a straight line, there would have to be something before God and something after God, as a line has a beginning and an end. A circle is infinite and can therefore have a beginning and end at any point. Genesis means beginnings. King James renders beginning singular, but in the original Hebrew it is a plural word: beginnings. The first verse of the Bible should read: "In the beginnings" or "In a beginning." It is not speaking of "the" beginning, but "a" beginning. In a circle, a beginning can be at any point, yet if the course of the circle is followed, the beginning will be the end, and the end will be the beginning. Beginnings and endings are at the same point. Judging by external perception, we will see beginnings and endings as a straight line. We begin here ← we end there →. This is not so in the realm of spirit; you end wherever you began. That's keeping your eye single and not walking in duality: the carnal way of judging by appearance, which brings a law of duality or double-mindedness. You can begin at any point and have lost nothing when the cycle is completed. That makes the entire circle beginning and ending, yet the circle has no beginning or ending at any point within itself.

With such new inventions as the Hubble Telescope, scientists have reached further and further into space discovering new galaxies and solar systems, seemingly without number. Space and matter were presumed to be unending. Today, however, scientists are persuaded that space actually curves in upon itself. Thus, a person starting out and continuing on, would eventually return to the point from which he started. There are no horizontal lines in any dimension that continue to go on and on, but everything will, at some point, bend or curve into a circular pattern.

In every person's journey, there is a point in which we, inherently, turn toward things pertaining to Spirit. This is what is meant by "every knee will bow and every tongue will confess". (Rom. 14:11) The spirit always returns back to God whether housed in a physical body or not. We get excited over the revelation of ultimate reconciliation, but in reality, it is a goal or an ultimate intention. It cannot be accomplished today, in a weekend, a week, a month or even a year. We must be careful not to be caught up in ultimate intentions. Most ministries that preach revelation knowledge represent ultimate intentions (goals, destiny). This is basically what we have heard so far. Our spirit rejoices when it hears these truths, because it does not know time, plus, it can rejoice at truth from any level, dimension or point in time. Time is relative. Spirit does not know the point of a beginning, middle or end, therefore it rejoices in the beginning, through the middle and unto the end. But, we have now come to a time and place that we must allow truth to meet us where we live. There is a bending in all of these things. The top of a circle represents the point where we came out of God. In your mind follow the pattern of a circle counterclockwise from the top.

We came out of God, have been progressing on in God, and have now come to the point of returning to God. As we come to the bottom of the circle, we reach a time where everything bottoms out. That is where we are in this generation. Everything has gone as far as it can go; or gone as low as it can, in this journey within the circle, which, is God's original blueprint.

Let's consider the place we have come to (the bottom of the circle), where everything has gone as low as it can in all natural and spiritual levels. This is the reason the religions of this world appear to be so effective. That which is seen and heard in the realms of religion is not the move of God. Do not be fooled or deceived by the things the multitudes of people are following. They appear to be successful because they are using the conditions of the world to manipulate the minds of masses of people with fear and confusion. Before religion could give the cure, they had to give the diagnosis. Before anyone would listen to their message of heaven, they had to have a hell. There had to be a hell bad enough to make you want to go to their heaven. Death, doom and destruction is preached to the point of literally producing the illnesses in the very ones who are found in their healing lines. A nervousness and worry takes over the minds of people who believe their loved ones have gone into eternity with no hope, to burn in the torments of hell fire. They have been taught the world is soon coming to an end, and the devil is taking over and multitudes will die without salvation. When the preachers come up with a solution (heaven), people take hold of it, not fully understanding it, because they are so desperate for anything that will give them peace of mind, even for a moment. They believe they are a dying species with no hope, only to be whisked away to some mystical city in the sky.

On the other side of the coin we have the ***awakened ones,*** who are on the opposite end of the extreme. Because of the lack of balance in revelation, they are sitting back doing nothing. Their attitude is that if God's going to do it anyway and it's all taken care of, then what do I have to worry about; I don't want any responsibility. We must find a place in the middle of these two extremes to understand that many of the things preached within the realms of religion can be brought into a higher level of revelation and transmuted to become constructive energy, rather than destructive. This is where evaluation of all levels begins to come into focus. One side sees only doom and destruction, while the other side sees only light and spirit. Both are refusing to face the reality of where man is in his outer world. It does not matter how much we know in our minds, our outer lives are portraying the same conditions and responses as the rest of humanity. We experience the same hurts, pains, doubts and insecurities, etc. This has been a great mystery to those who have received high revelations. The question asked more often is, "Why?" Why are we yet subject to the limitations of human suffering?

We came out of God, and have been progressing through different levels of God as tremendous truths have been revealed. This has been in a downward motion, which again portrays a circle in your mind that starts at the top and follows downward to the left. Although we have been on the pathway of destiny, it has been in a downward motion. The ascension has only been an inner experience, and for the most part, has not effected our external lives. Until now this has been according to the plan, but things are changing as we come to the bottom of the circle. Now we are making a sharp turn, beginning our return or ascension back to God, which is upward. Ascension is when we no longer continue on a downward motion. At this point it is not only an inner raising, but even now the body is being caught up into the reality of the revelations that we have seen on the first half of our journey. As we return to God, (not backwards, but forward and upward) the revelations will be personified and manifest into the flesh, and the word God has given will be made flesh. I am not speaking of immortality, but life (life in the flesh as it is raised to the level of spirit) that will bring tremendous change to the outer world.

When we speak of returning, some respond by saying, "Don't take me back I'm going on. I don't care what anyone says I'm going all the way to God. I've come too far to turn back now." Again, we must understand that returning to God is not going backwards, but forward. We stand at a crucial point, for as we fulfill the first half of our journey and begin to make the curve returning to God, we have come to a time when certain principles that have governed our lives in the past are now fulfilled. In the first half of our journey, we walked under the Sovereignty of God. Let's examine the principles contained within sovereignty to understand why it was necessary.

When a person first comes to the awakening of God through what has been called his salvation experience, he is in a state of innocence, because he is an infant in Christ. One only remains in a state of innocence as long as he is ignorant or without knowledge. Adam was innocent in the garden before he partook of the knowledge of good and evil. Therefore he was ignorant. A newborn baby is innocent, not because it has knowledge to make it innocent, but because it hasn't any knowledge in the outer sense of the world. Parents move in sovereignty over the life of an infant in caring for them, making all their decisions and expecting nothing in return. They are the survival of the infant. But each stage of maturity in the development of a child brings out a new instinct in the nature of parenting. When a child is an infant, the parents feed them and change their diapers out of love knowing they cannot do these things for themselves. As the child grows and develops, the nature of the parent changes. They begin to do everything with a purpose of allowing the child to learn to do things themselves.

God takes care of his infants in a wonderful way, but growth and maturity brings out a new response in his nature. He will continue to do for them, only now they must pay attention as he teaches them to make their own decisions and govern their own lives. He teaches them these things through knowledge, and sooner or later everyone must grow out of the state of innocence. It is growth and maturity that brings a fulfillment to the sovereignty of God. Once we have fulfilled the realm of sovereignty we are ready to enter the realm of freewill. That part of man that does not want to grow up and take responsibility begins to protest and attempt to remain in a state of innocence, locked into a principle that must be fulfilled. The mind begins to shout out its revelation of sovereignty, not realizing that it can cause a lack of sensitivity and obedience to present truth.

The majority of people come from religious backgrounds steeped in teachings of freewill. We were taught that God only responds to what man chooses to do of his own freewill. If he chooses Jesus, he goes to heaven; if not, then he has chosen hell. This makes man's freewill the total author of his destiny. In the midst of this belief, the light of revelation knowledge broke through and revealed the sovereignty of God in the lives of all men. We were taken totally out of freewill and placed totally into the sovereignty of God, as we declared that all things are working after the counsel of his will. (Eph. 1:11) Religion brought us into an extreme at one end, and God will meet us at the other end. It is out of the extreme of two points that God makes known true balance. One cannot know the balance between two points until there are two points in which to find the middle or the balance. We have come totally out of the extremity of freewill as presented by religion to the extremity of sovereignty as presented by revelation. We are to be given the privilege of finding the balance between the two points to become true worshippers, who worship the Father in spirit and in Truth.

The brightness of the light of revelation blinded us, bringing a deception that we had no freewill left, causing us to think we were robots who could do nothing but what we were programmed to do. This has produced an attitude that projects: *I don't have to grow or mature for nothing is up to me, it's all up to God. It does not matter what I do or not do, God will eventually have his way. I don't have to think or make any decisions. If you don't like what you see, don't blame me. God is responsible.* At one time the devil was our scapegoat; then God became our scapegoat. I suggest we give this some serious contemplation. We came out of the system no longer thinking we needed any structure in our lives. Anything that had to do with structure or organization became taboo and old order. Any lack was God's fault, because man's will is totally governed by God.

The pendulum has swung from one extreme to the other, and neither end has produced anything but a dilemma of total confusion. God did not bring us out of freewill, structure, organization, form or law, because they were not needed. He brought us out of religion's way of doing these things to show us His ways. God has always been a God of order and structure. We see this all through the scriptures. In throwing everything away and not allowing anything to replace it, we have literally created a purgatory. This has placed us in a dimension of an in between heaven and hell state. One-day heaven is great, the next hell has a hold of us yet we are not in either one, but have the mixture of both manifesting in our lives. We live in, an off and on, up and down, in and out experience. Yes, we have learned how to occupy this place with a certain glorious style, but only because we halt between two opinions: we're never quite sure who is responsible, (us or God) thus we are forced to deceive ourselves into a mental delusion that surely God is in control.

Let me again emphasize the fact, it is growth and maturity that has brought us to this place. Knowledge has freed us from innocence, requiring that we evaluate where we are and where are we going from here. At this level of understanding, we have progressed in knowledge to understand the reconciliation of all things, which is not an ultimate level; but a particular fulfillment of a plateau. When one comes to understand God's plan and purpose: his end and ultimate intention, **then** God, steps back for a season. At this point of progression and development, God steps back to see what we will do with the things we have learned. It is at the point in the circle where the curve is made to begin our ascension and return to God; that sovereignty is fulfilled, and God returns us to our will. The accuser of the brethren, that religious part of our mind, steps in and says, "Sorry, I believe all things work after the counsel of his will." *It is* the counsel of His will to return you to your own will to choose to make your will aligned with His will. Know that His will is to release you and see what you will do with what you have received in the first half of your journey.

We stand at a crossroads between two decisions: to evolve to the next dimension or to physically destroy ourselves. The prophet Joel says in Joel 3:14: "Multitudes, multitudes are in the valley of decision: for the day of the Lord is near in the valley of decision." In spite of the fact that many people are terrified to make decisions, decisions are healthy. We have all cried out for the maturity of God to manifest in our lives. The first sign of maturity is the inner ability to make decisions aligned to God's purpose for you. It is not normal for parents to make decisions for their son or daughter all their life. Decisions are only made during the years they are not capable of making them for themselves. We teach them how to make decisions, then step back and give them the freedom to make choices, with a deep hope that we have done our best in teaching them. How much more does our heavenly Father search the earth today to find those who have learned his ways to the point of being able to stand and enhance him as they express the nature he has invested in them.

We have come out of God and walked through many years of revelation and enlightenment which has taken us through a process of dehumanization, (taking the "hue[67]" out of the human to make a new creation man). It was the sovereignty of God that directed our footsteps in the right direction to hear a word that would free us from human consciousness imposed on us by religion. It was not our good works that caused this to happen, nor did our evil works prevent it from happening. It was the sovereignty of God's will for our lives. We have fulfilled the first half of our journey, which has simply been a journey through revelation knowledge. Following the circle counterclockwise from the top, we have now come to the bottom and are ready to make the curve to begin our ascension, returning back into God. This is the most important part of our journey thus far, and the most dangerous. It is at this point of the curve that God steps back to see what each one will do with what he have been given thus far. There has not been a generation of people upon the earth who have ever made this curve.[68]

I wonder if we realize the magnitude of having the privilege to be the first to make the curve and begin the return. I am sure there are some who would wonder at such a statement as this and would ask by what authority do you say this is the first generation? If there had been a former generation who qualified, at this point, there would be people on the earth manifesting the totality of a resurrected life.

We would see the personification and manifestation of the great revelation given to many in former generations. Today, some are surprised to learn other generations have received many of the great revelations being made known today. Many books were written hundreds of years ago revealing the mysteries and secrets you and I have been privileged

---

67 *A lesser color, particular shade or tint*
68 *Individuals may have, but not a collective group*

to know. This is by no means the first time great revelations have been given to people walking on the earth.

Qualification is a word that must now be dropped into our consciousness. In it lies a very important part of our sonship that is totally unfamiliar to those who have walked under the banner of sovereignty. It does not matter if one is predestined and predetermined; there is a point of qualification. Jesus was predestined and predetermined, yet had to qualify to become a manifested Son of God. The scriptures make it clear that he looked to the cross with joy, because he understood the things that were before him. He was a Son of God, in the earth realm, for thirty years, but during that time he was not a manifested Son. The greatest thing Jesus did for the first thirty years of his life was astound a few people in the synagogues with the things that came out of his mouth. He did not heal or perform any miracles. He did not raise the dead, walk on the water, cast out devils, or multiply loaves and fishes. We see this same pattern at work in the sons who are in the earth today. The only manifestation displayed is what comes out of our mouths. We have all asked why. The answer lies in qualification.

Those who have walked through the first half of their journey have come to a place where they, too, must qualify, just as Jesus had to qualify in the garden. The scriptures speak of Jesus as one who came in the volume of the book to do the will of God. (Heb. 10:7) He knew and understood God's will for his life. The will or sovereignty of God governed him before his birth and throughout his life. Yet, the day came when he arrived at a place of finally dealing with his own will, freewill if you please. Jesus could not go to the Father until he dealt with his freewill. When Jesus looked at his will in the garden, he had to say, "It is not my will to be nailed to a cross and shed my blood." In his own words he said: "Father, if thou be willing, remove this cup from me: nevertheless, not *my will*, but thine be done." (Luke 22:42) It was at this point that Jesus aligned his own will with the will of the Father, and his will and God's will became **ONE**. That was maturity and the qualification God was looking for from his Son. Jesus could not be released to finish his mission until he was mature enough to go into the world and do exactly, of his own freewill and choosing, what God had purposed. God's sons in the earth today cannot fulfill their destiny until they have brought their own will into the light and of the revelation they have been given, aligning their will with God's will. Qualification is not by sovereignty - it is by freewill.

We must open our eyes to see how beautifully freewill fits into the will of God. At the point where your will is aligned with God's will, you begin to respond to God in a new and unique way. You no longer do his will because you have to, or because you are programmed to, but because you have willingly, of your own choosing, made your will his will. Out of this union, a praise will be birthed, as expressions of love to God such as we have never experienced. God has been longing for this sound to touch His heart. That's the sound that has been missing from praise among the elect that has caused much frustration. Praise and worship, as we have known it, has become empty and lifeless. Something has been missing that we have not understood. Many have turned from any form of praise and worship because of this. We can now understand, this praise has come out of a part of what was predestined and preordained. As predestination was fulfilled, praise from that level no longer gave forth that certain sound we have all longed for. We shall see a new praise spring forth. The method or verbal sounds may not change, but the sound will contain a new vibration, a new frequency that will touch the heart of the Father causing him to step out and inhabit this praise, because people are bringing it as an offering of their ***own will***. It will be this praise that will birth a new move, and a new manifestation of God into the earth. This praise will cause a people to rise into the higher places of union, revelation and substance to become ***one*** with that which we have been taught as we sat at his feet. We see a beautiful picture of man's freewill in God's words to the children of Israel:

> "And the Lord spoke unto Moses saying, Speak unto the children of Israel, that they bring me an offering: of every man that giveth it willingly with his heart, ye shall take my offering. And let them make me a sanctuary, that I may dwell among them." (Ex. 25:1, 2, 8)

Israel was blessed with great substance as they came out of the land of Egypt. God told Moses to take an offering from all those who would give it willingly. The offering consisted of gold, silver, brass, blue and purple scarlet, fine linen, and many other possessions that had been placed in their hands. We can liken these things to the great wealth of revelation knowledge that God has given to us today. Again, God is saying, "Bring me an offering of every man that giveth it willingly." It is of great importance to realize God only desired those things to be given back to him by those who were willing. The children of Israel wanted to use their possessions to adorn themselves, not realizing the tremendous importance they were destined for. What a parallel to many sons in the earth today, as they come to a place of being blessed to hear from God; they make earrings of gold and parade before the people saying, "Look at me, I can hear from God." You must be willing to take off the golden earring and give it back to God; but it **must** be given with a willing heart.

As I have already stated, the point in our journey where we make the curve beginning our ascension and return back to God is a most dangerous place. Sovereignty will no longer hold you in the perfect plan of God for your life. As you are returned to freewill, you must be the one who makes the curve to begin the ascension and return back to God. At the point of the curve, one can begin to go out (➔) and not up, leaving the pure flow of the circularity of spirit. If this happens, the mind can bring deception that you are going up, when in reality you are going out. This is the beginning of "a way that seemeth right unto man; but the end thereof are the ways of death." (Prov. 14:12) God is faithful, and at this point his mercy steps in, for this death is the mercy of God. Man will not always continue on this way that seemeth right, for any direction he chooses to take will eventually return him to God. This is where reconciliation comes in, for, "Thine own wickedness shall correct thee, and thy backslidings shall reprove thee." (Jer. 2:19)

By this time, some may be thinking, "What difference does it make if I make the turn and go up or if I go out? Why worry about it if the salvation of all men is secure." This attitude comes from a lack of understanding. The thing that is totally secure for all men is that they will be saved and returned to God. "…and the spirit shall return to God who gave it." (Ecc. 12:7) That's one side of the coin, but we also need to look at the other side. When a person reaches that place where he has to make a choice of whether to align his will with God's, and does not choose to do so, something can be lost that will never be regained. We can read this in the words of Paul:

> "For other foundation can no man lay than that is laid, which is Jesus Christ. Now if any man build upon this foundation gold, silver, precious stones, wood, hay, stubble; Every man's work shall be made manifest: for the day shall declare it, because it shall be revealed by fire; and the fire shall try every man's work of what sort it is. If any man's work abide which he hath built thereupon, he shall receive a reward. If any man's work shall be burned, he shall *suffer loss*; but he himself shall be saved, yet as by fire." (I Cor. 3:11-15)

In this scripture we see six ingredients. Six is the number of man, thus each man must pass through the purification process seen in this principle. The gold, silver and precious stones are non-consumable and speak of God's nature, redemption, and revelation knowledge. Wood, hay, and stubble speak of religious mental efforts that make God's word of no effect. All of man's works shall be manifest in the day he reaches the place of qualification by freewill. It is not a calendar day, nor a day set by number or year; but it is the day when one comes to the age of responsibility and approaches a certain level of consciousness. It will then be declared by becoming an expression within man's nature and no longer just a revelation. At this point in progression, all works shall be openly declared in every man; whether it be the hay, wood and stubble, or the gold, silver, and precious stones. Fire is the thing that will cause this declaration to take place. Over the years, we have heard a lot of things concerning the fire of God, yet none of them have brought an open declaration and manifestation in our lives. The fire spoken of is the righteous of God.

Let's consider the subject of judgment. We have discarded judgment in an attempt not to condemn, and in an honest effort to allow every man the freedom to be who he is, and do whatever he has to in his walk with God. When you are able to transcend the law and legalism of religion that passes condemnation and on every one who does not live by their rules and regulations, you have entered a wonderful place of great freedom and liberty. Like many other things, however, it has swung to an extreme and is totally out of balance. There is another side to we have not given much thought to. In the first chapter of Isaiah we read of a time when God will restore judges and counselors to redeem Zion with righteous judgment. Afterward, Israel will be called a faithful city; the city of righteousness. (Is. 1:26) In the eleventh chapter of Isaiah we read of a branch that will be endowed with the spirit of wisdom, understanding, counsel, might, knowledge and the fear of the Lord. He will be of quick understanding and shall judge; but not by the seeing of the eye, nor the hearing of the ear. The fire that will reveal every man's works is the restoration of true judgment. (Is. 11:1-2) We are going to see the ministry of a judge raised up in our midst who will walk in wisdom, and speak a word that will settle situations that have plagued many for most of their lives.

God's people, who have walked in high places of revelation knowledge, have been so afraid of judging and condemning that it has caused a loss of true discernment. There is a great need for discernment to be restored to the hearts of God's people. Does the scripture not state that we shall judge the world? Read it in the words of Paul:

> "Do ye not know that the saints shall judge the world? And if the world shall be judged by you, are ye unworthy to judge the smallest matters? Know ye not that we shall judge angels? How much more things that pertain to this life?" (I Cor. 6:2,3)

Let us not think that God will turn the government of this world over to a people lacking in discernment and wisdom, to render a judgment unto life.

In the ranks of "God's sons", we have come to a time that "every man does what is right in his own eyes." (Judges 17:6) Many feel they have not needed judgment or counsel, saying to themselves, "After all, God is in all things, and nothing could happen, unless it was the will of God." How we have suffered in our extremities, but, at last, the day is upon us that every man's work shall be declared by fire, and out of this we shall see an order come to our lives that has long been needed.

David Hulse, D.D.

You can suffer loss, although you will be saved[69]. Every time one goes out on the path that seemeth right, he will experience death. This is not necessarily a physical death, but can be the same kind of death Adam walked through. Adam, even though he was dead to spirit and to God, lived over nine hundred years after he was pronounced dead in a flesh body. God allowed him to be turned over to his own mind and his own thinking. Perhaps, the greatest tragedy is when one experiences this kind of death, he carries with him into darkness the revelations he has received, which are void of the leading of spirit. Revelation without spiritual direction can become the most destructive force in the earth, or in the Universe. No man who has ever influenced this world was stupid. Those who have influenced generation after generation with their philosophies and beliefs were men who possessed great knowledge. The basis of Marxism, Nazism, etc. came from men who diligently studied the esoterical principles in may different religions, including Christianity, and used them to manipulate masses of people for destructive purposes.

The most dangerous people to deal with are those who have received great revelation knowledge, and were once under the direction of spirit, but have moved out of a spirit flow. The carnal mind begins to preach revelation from the origins of flesh and not spirit. The spirit element is taken totally out of their message, and revelation is used to produce for the flesh; because until the mind is redeemed and returned to spirit it can only produce for the flesh. The flesh desires to have children just as the spirit wants to be productive and reproduce. These people will eventually be reconciled back to God, but they will suffer loss of something that can never be restored. The loss is a qualification for places of governmental authority and leadership in the kingdom. They will become subjects to the government of God. The scripture is very clear about the hierarchy of God's government. I realize we are not accustomed to this kind of thinking, but we have entered a serious hour in which we must understand certain principles to find life.

God must speak plainly to cause an awakening from complacency and the relaxed attitude that thoughts and actions do not matter. Although God has shown us his ultimate love: he can and will, if necessary, take something away if it is for our higher good. This concept

---

69   I Corinthians 3:15

cannot be clearly understood by those who yet perceive God to be vindictive and without mercy. Love must sometimes bring correction, judgment and pain. The so-called "Sons of God" have become spoiled, wanting their way, and thinking God should give them whatever they want, because they are his elect. A true understanding of election will not make one feel they are superior or of greater importance than another. Every man, at some point, will choose to awaken. If you feel chosen, it is because you have elected to respond to the call of God to be enlightened at this time. Election is a place, not a people and is only by sovereignty and grace. **It is not by works, lest any man should boast.**

There is a spiritual genetic code locked up in every man's spirit. When man passes through life at a certain level of consciousness, the code is activated by his willingness to become God's availability in the earth. An awakening process begins, moving him into a position to choose his election period.

Revelation brings with it a feeling of self-sufficiency, a feeling of having need of nothing or no one outside of self. How soon one forgets that Lucifer said he would be like the Most High, and then was cast down to an earth level. There is a revelation that tells us we are gods,[70] Elohiym, co-creators, yet if we read the words of the Psalmist carefully, we also find though we are god's representatives, We are all children of the Most High. (Psalms 82:6) Can you understand why Jesus said, "Suffer the little children to come unto me...for of such is the kingdom of heaven...whosoever shall not receive the kingdom as a little child, he shall not enter therein." (Mark 10:14, 15) We must return to our Father as a child in total dependence upon him, not leaning to our own abilities, sufficiencies or revelations. It is the desire of our Father's heart to give us the reality of all we have seen by revelation. Yet his great wisdom requires it not be given to one who would channel it through his own mental consciousness, which distorts and twists the very substance of which he is made.

In spite of all the revelations we have received, we must return to God and refuse to be a god unto ourselves. The scripture has declared: "Ye are gods." When one comes to this awakening, he can go out and attempt to be god: doing away with Jesus, doing away with any god

---

70 *God's representatives in the earth*

except for the one within. Many confuse the god of religion with the true and living One. When their god of religion dies, they feel there is no god except for them. All the images of God are gone, and they find the presence of God within. They discover they came out of spirit and did not begin with the physical body. This is all truth, but it has carried with it one major deception, for it contains the fruit of error. The fruit of error is **exaltation**, the fruit of spirit is **humility**. Jesus did not come into the world to declare himself. He continually told the people not to look at him, for he did not speak his own words nor do his own works, but only what he heard of his Father. He pointed man to God with the confession: he could of his own self do nothing. Jesus represents the Spirit coming into flesh. He was God manifested in and through flesh, but his flesh was not God.

Religion has made a God out of the man Jesus, in spite of his explicit instructions that they were not to worship him, but to worship the Father in spirit and truth. Two thousand years down the road, they still do not know him as he is, but only know him as he was in the flesh of the man of Galilee. There is no reality in worshipping any man's flesh, be it Jesus or anyone else. Today we see the same thing happening all over again as man attempts to make the flesh body of Christ in the earth today to be God. It is time to talk plainly of these things.

We found out we came out of God and are spirit just as he is: made of his same substance and in his likeness. What a wonderful revelation to know that Christ *In Me* is the hope of glory and Christ **As Me** is the glory. Yet, there is a principle contained in all of these things we must be careful not to overlook. To everything there is a purpose. In the scriptures we see many different facets of God, and within each facet there was a desire to find those of like facet. Jesus the Son of God found it necessary to fall into the ground and die so he might produce more sons. In Psalms 110, we find the Lord talking to his lords. In Psalms 82, God is judging among his gods. The principle being, the son wanted other sons to communicate with. God looked for gods, and the Lord looked for lords. How can any of these things be manifested from the level of their existence to that which is not at an equal level?

The religious world does not know the Son of God, because they have not found their own sonship to know him through. Deep always calls unto deep, and like always calls unto like. Only those who have awakened to who they are can know him as he is. No man can come to the Father, but by the Son. Receiving revelation of our sonship became the entrance for us to meet God the Father. It is through an awakening of your God-likeness you are able to communicate and know God at the level he is. Until this happens, God has to condense himself down into revelation. That is only the beginning, for revelation has brought us inside the house to find him so we may know him.

Cleansing Of The High Place

There is a realm or dimension man can enter into where the heavens open. In this dimension, he is able to see and hear great mysteries and secrets of God. This is an awesome and wondrous place, yet it is a dangerous place. Man's first encounter with death occurred because of his great thirst for knowledge. The scriptures clearly state that knowledge puffed up; and though we have all knowledge and understand all mysteries, we are nothing without love. (I Cor. 8:1; 13:2) The scriptures also instruct one to seek knowledge with all his heart, for without knowledge man is destroyed. (Ho. 4:6)

The things that are the most valuable can often become the most dangerous, if not kept in the right and proper prospective. The danger lies in the fact that when one is caught up into spiritual revelations, he is often unable to walk in the reality of what was revealed on a day-to-day basis. Walking in the dimension of an open heaven is a type of rapture, as we are taken away from the consciousness of humanity and allowed to view God's plan. Webster gives a most interesting definition of the word rapture: "a state or experience of being carried away by overwhelming emotions, a mystical experience in which the spirit is exalted to a knowledge of divine things." This is exactly what revelation does: it enables one, by spirit, to literally look upon knowledge that is divinely inspired by God.

David Hulse, D.D.

Most of the people in the earth today have heard all their lives that God is cruel and vindictive. The result of this has caused great fears and insecurities, plus a feeling it is impossible to live up to the standards expected by God. When the light began to shine out of darkness showing man his true standing with God, it was overwhelming, and in the beginning brought great joy and freedom. However, this only lasts for a season. Then one begins to look at all the things he has heard; and without realizing it, begins to depend upon his great revelations and not upon God. A different kind of guilt, insecurity and condemnation arises; and one begins to wonder what is wrong. A part of the mind (ego) begins to say, "What's wrong with you? You know better than this." The mind then begins to search through the knowledge it has acquired for answers, but it is a search for greater knowledge and not a search for God.

This is the condition we see in the earth today among those who have walked in a place of high revelation. Some are again becoming desperate as they are forced to admit all the knowledge they have been given has not changed their external world. Out of this condition a cry has arisen that is touching the heart of the Father. Read it in the words of Jeremiah:

> "A voice was heard upon the high places, weeping and supplication of the children of Israel: for ***they*** have perverted their way, and they have forgotten the Lord their God. Return ye backsliding children and I will heal your backslidings..." (Jer. 3:21, 22)

There is a voice being heard from the high places of revelation. It is not the cry of creation; it is a different cry. People are awakening to the realization that unless they move with their knowledge by the spirit, it will become perverted, bringing death and not life. All who progress to this point in their awakening will come to this place. Revelation is given to bring man to God, not to become his god. It is not the knowledge one is given that will bring life, but what is contained within that knowledge.

There is a sound coming forth from those who are dedicated to God's purpose and therefore, touching the very heart of the Father.

It is not their desire to usurp God's place but to be God's availability upon the earth[71].

> "Therefore the redeemed of the Lord shall return, and come with singing unto Zion; and everlasting joy shall be upon their heads: they shall obtain gladness and joy; and sorrow and mourning shall flee away." (Is. 51:11)

The redeemed of the Lord are returning; not the dope addict, not the prostitute, not the alcoholic, nor the so-called sinner. It is the redeemed: those who understand and know their union and completeness in God. They have entered the high realms of knowledge about God by revelation and are now returning unto God. To those who understand that their spirit has been joined unto the Lord to become one spirit, the call goes forth, "Return unto God."

Why are they returning and for what purpose? They are returning to God to, once again, make him their focus. They are returning with singing, however, it is not a song they have learned; but a song of higher vibration that cannot be expressed in earthly language. Many have become weary with singing and praise; but we must realize as we begin this great ascension and return to God, singing will break forth. However, it will come from a higher vibration and be released into the outer world, becoming the vehicle to birth a new praise in the hearts of the redeemed. This new praise will touch every level of creation. This kind of singing will reach into the hearts of people and plant a seed of a higher word. People will be drawn into the high places of God as this new song comes forth from Zion[72]: releasing a higher vibration, a higher frequency, a higher form of spirit to become an availability into the outer world. This will be expressed in and through those with a sensitive and obedient heart who arise and return unto God.

The redeemed of the Lord are returning with everlasting joy upon their heads. That which is upon their heads is the great revelations given by God, but it is only on the head, and not expressed into the outer world. As we return, we shall obtain the things that are only on the head. We've had a revelation of joy, but now joy shall be obtained. Everything that has been in the realm of revelation knowledge can be

71 *Exodus 7:1*
72 Zion represents the highest place of the temple in Jerusalem.

obtained as we return unto God. We must now align ourselves with the direction of spirit, for we will not obtain the expression of anything that has been seen thus far by continuing on the path of one revelation after the other. Knowledge has taken preeminence over God. We must return and again make God our focus.

We are yet to hear God speak plainly. Up to this point he has only spoken in degrees in order to prepare us to hear what he really has to say. It is his great mercy and foresight that is reaching out and creating a desire within the depths of our being to stop following only the path of knowledge. We have come to a time that we must evaluate everything that has been given up to this point. We have been given a part of God's plan of healing for all the world. We have caught a glimpse of a people who can overcome sickness, disease, old age and death itself. We have laid hold of great knowledge that God has so graciously given. Yet in so doing, I am afraid we have thrown away many principles that are a part of our foundation.

It was necessary to lay aside the traditions of men that had made the word of God of no effect. Yet, we must realize that each principle holds a vital key to full salvation. As we return to God, he will take each principle we have learned over the years and show us the purity it contains. Paul instructed us to leave the principles of the doctrines of Christ that we might go on to perfection. (Hebrews 6:1-3) However, if we take a close look at the six principles of the doctrine of Christ, we must admit we have not known the full effect of their purpose. We have only known man's interpretations. We must now ask the Father what he has to say concerning repentance from dead works, faith toward God, the doctrine of baptisms, laying on of hands, resurrection of the dead and eternal judgment. Hidden behind the letter of all these principles lies a great wealth yet to be unlocked and incorporated into our walk with God. Please understand I am not suggesting we go back to any degree we have known in the past, but find the truth contained within each one.

The scripture speaks of bearing fruit; some thirty-fold, some sixty-fold, and some one hundred-fold. When a step is taken in progression from the thirty-fold to the sixty-fold, it takes the fullness of the thirty to make up the fullness of the sixty. If you throw away the first thirty, you only have thirty remaining. The next step is the one hundred-fold, but again it takes the fullness of the sixty-fold to complete the one hundred-fold, or there is only forty left. If the thirty is discarded when you enter the sixty-fold realm, and the sixty is discarded when you enter the one hundred-fold, there is only a ten-fold left. This explains the great lacking in those who have entered the realms of high revelation. Every time a new principle is revealed, everything else is thrown away. All that remains is a revelation: a beautiful revelation of great truth, but only a ten-fold manifestation of fruit, which is love, joy, peace, temperance, meekness, etc. (Gal. 5:22-23) It is time to awaken to the fact we are on a journey of progressive truth, and it takes the fullness of each part to complete the whole, which becomes greater than its parts.

As the redeemed of the Lord return, they shall obtain what is upon their heads, and all sorrow and mourning shall flee away. It matters not if it is salvation, the baptism of the Holy Spirit, praise, worship or prayer; all of these things contain within them the heart and purity of their substance, a true reality that must be ministered to the ends of the earth to bring salvation to all men. There has been a great need to turn aside from the watered down interpretations of these things that have caused us to throw the baby out with the bath water. I am not suggesting that we return to any former day, or any former way; but we must become God's availability to flow out to all men at whatever level **they** may be. We must evaluate our very foundation and allow God to reveal the pureness of each level. This will produce a manifestation of God in the flesh, and not just a revelation of God in the flesh.

The cry is going forth for the redeemed of the Lord to "awaken as in the ancient days, in the generations of old." (Is. 51:9) The redeemed of the Lord are not to awaken and return to former experiences, but they are to awaken to the vein of truth which is concealed in spirit. All realms we have walked through have been tainted by religion, but let me again emphasize that within each is a piece of the puzzle: a part of the pattern. The truth of each realm we have walked through must be gathered and harmonized. This will cause us to obtain the goal that has been set before us.

> "That the generation to come might know them, even
> the children which shall be born; who should arise and
> declare them to their children: That they might set their

> hope in God, and not forget the works of God, but keep his commandments: And might not be as their fathers, a stubborn and rebellious generation; a generation that set not their heart aright, and whose spirit was not steadfast with God." (Ps. 78:6-9)

Give ear to what the spirit would say to the church. Many of the liberties and freedoms that have been found through the vehicle of revelation knowledge have become great bondage. People talk about their liberty so much that it becomes clear they are in bondage to their liberty, and could never enter other realms to minister a word that is needed. Many are so free from the system and from Babylon[73] that their freedom keeps them from flowing in areas that they themselves once stood in.

I am not referring to the twisted teaching of man's doctrines, but to those things that make up our foundation and brought us to where we are today. Allow yourself to stop for a moment and remember a few of the experiences you had with God before coming into the deeper revelations about God. Remember the Holy Spirit revival when people ran to the altars to give their hearts to God because of pure Holy Spirit conviction; and being filled with the Holy Spirit and walking in an awesome presence for days and weeks afterwards. Sometimes we speak of these things a little softly, because we don't want the newer ones to hear us speaking **past order**. We've gotten so high we don't dare deal with these things, especially from the pulpit. We have our own wonderful personal memories of how we were saved, filled with the spirit and baptized in water. Yet we have refused to give those, who have come into a relationship with God through knowledge, the opportunity to experience these things, because they are considered a past order.

In the depth of my being I hear these words, "Who are you that though you have experienced these things you won't let the children? You who have enjoyed my blessings and the works of my hands, who are you to hide from the generations to come the praises of God?" The scripture above, from Psalms 78, speaks of the children to come who should arise and declare the works of God. This speaks of both natural and spiritual children. For the most part we have not seen too much

---

[73] Babylon represents religious rhetoric to keep the masses in confusion.

focus on the teaching of our children. It's old order to take the time to give them a foundation. We must ask ourselves, would we hide from them the things that have given us the strength to stand upon the solid rock of our foundation in the face of all adversity? Will we allow the revelation, that God will reconcile all things back unto himself, to lure us into complacency and apathy? Will we let this keep us from taking the responsibility of allowing an availability for those who hunger and thirst for the great experience of salvation?

There is a part of every man's salvation that he must be awakened to so that he might stand sure and steadfast in the faith once delivered. There is no new faith. The same faith that was once delivered to the saints is the faith that should be preached today. It is time to return unto God and allow him to show us the true faith, not this mind believing that is preached under the cloak of faith within the realms of religion today. The true faith of God is not putting a picture of a Cadillac or a Lincoln Continental on the bathroom mirror so you can get it into your mind and draw it to you. The faith given by God is a faith that caused the early Christians to stand in the face of the adversary and never lose the joy in their hearts, the song on their lips or the dance in their feet. They had something far beyond the realm of positive thinking or name it and claim it thinking. Only God can endow one with his faith. It cannot be taught from any degree of knowledge. Without faith there is no hope. Our hope must be returned to God rather than to some revelation about him.

In vs. 8 of Ps. 78 it speaks of the fathers who were stubborn and rebellious. This can be seen among those who become stubborn and rebellious about the knowledge they have heard up to this point. They hide from the children anything that doesn't line up with their new-found order. There is a rebelliousness among the so-called elect that gives forth a know-it-all attitude. This seems to happen at every level of progression of truth. It is an attitude that refuses to be changed. "God spoke it to me, that's the way it is, and you'll come my way! I'll have nothing to do with anything else!" This attitude is in the high places among those who, with all their high and mighty revelations, have not set their heart aright. It is time for an alignment between man's heart and the revelations he has heard. The greater the revelation, the less stability is seen. Commitment to God and his creation is many times lost. With all the revelation there is still talk, gossip, criticism and prejudice. Revelation has not changed a thing. These things have been brought with us right out of Babylon and taken into the high places.

God has "established a testimony in Jacob, and appointed a law in Israel." (Ps. 78:5) There is a word that has been established within a people that they will never be the same as they were when walking under the traditions of man-made laws. There is an order: a level that can never be left behind. Because of this you can now return unto God and evaluate the experiences of salvation. You will take the place you are established in, back to the places you have left. I am not saying go back to their churches, or stand in their pulpits, for the place you are to return to and stand in is God. It is not necessary to go back into the systems God has called you out of, but you are to stand upon the principles established within you which gave life and reality, and placed you on a sure foundation. We are to go back to that place in us, yet never leave the place God has brought us to. Heaven and earth are passing away; the old and the new are leaving. There will be no old order or new order. There will only be God's order. That which is ministered will be by the unction of spirit in a freshness of the *now*, to meet needs at any and every level. I've watched multitudes on television go forward to give their hearts to God. The question came to me, "How long has it been since you've given anyone the opportunity to come and accept me in the experience of salvation?" "But, we're not into that Lord, that's old order." Then God spoke something to me that caused a rude awakening: "Because no opportunity is given in the high place for people to come to me for salvation, you are causing them to come through the door religion presents, and be taught the traditions and doctrines of men. You are causing them to repeatedly experience the bondage's and imprisonments of religion just as you had to do. Consider this: Can you see the great need for a place to be made in the high place for people to find the God of salvation and be taught the reality of me?" Incline your ear — who is he talking to? He is talking to you, his elect, and his first fruits in the earth — incline your ear for I have something to say to you. God has established a testimony and appointed a law within a people so they can go to any level, yet never leave the level he has brought them to by revelation knowledge and understanding.

We have not been permitted to walk into perfection because we have to continually deal with people who came to salvation through the traditions of religion. We spend years undoing what we have been taught before we can begin to get close to what God is saying today. It is time to give an opportunity for people to come and find the Lord from those in high places so they can be taught the true Jesus; not Jesus as he was 2000 years ago, but as he is in the power of his resurrection. Let's be honest, many that shout "amen" the loudest to revelation knowledge and declare themselves to be the hope for the world, have not shaken off the bondage's imposed by the traditions of men.

Every time we have attained to a new perception of the truth, man has attempted to organize it into another religion. The last thing we need is another new religion. It is time for all fences to come down at this time of change and transformation in order to extend the light to all people at every level. We are His "earthen vessels" through whom He shall pour forth the treasures of His light. It is time to go beyond names, tags and titles; and stop stereotyping, realizing we can go anywhere and still remain who we are in the place God has brought us. It is time to turn the hearts of the people back to an experience of God and not just a hope in revelation. Can you understand how easy it is to take the children and make them think their hope is in what they've been taught and never be given the privilege of a personal relationship with the Christ within?

It is time for a recycling process to bring all things, both old and new, into the realms we have caught a glimpse of by revelation, so we might see where each fits in its proper perspective in the whole of truth. In the natural, there are specific times reproduction is more feasible than other times. The same is true in the realm of spirit. There is a spiritual cycle, a place when there can be a conception of your revelation. Until then, it just remains as head knowledge. Everything must be harmonized and synchronized properly to bring about conception in the heart from where the issues[74] of life proceed. There is a great urgency to understand that hearing is not enough, for there is another step, another level beyond hearing. We cannot stop just because we have the ability to hear. We must return and cry out for the Most High to overshadow his word and bring forth the manifestation of the sons of God. There

---

74 *Issues represent the spiritual children that are the manifestations of the outer conditions of our life.*

is a responsibility that comes with the ability to hear and perceive the deeper things of God. This responsibility is to bring revelation out of the realm of knowledge and into the realm of reality, by turning our focus back to God.

It is wonderful to have inspiration to hear the things God speaks, but if heard right they can only turn us back to God. People, who can only hear intellectually, make revelation become the god that once again blinds them from seeing the reality of the God within. I have observed when people become more attached to a belief, it keeps them from experiencing the very thing they believe in. We need the God of our revelation, not another revelation about God. It is the Father who seeketh you to worship Him in spirit and in truth

God has brought many out of the bondage of religious doctrines, laws and legalism that have brought death and condemnation to them, to walk into a place rich with revelation knowledge. We often leave a gathering with our houses full, but God would say: "…when thou shalt have eaten and be full, then beware least thou forget the Lord…[75]." As people continue on the path of knowledge and revelation, it is sometimes easy to forget God, and replace him with things like language, mysteries, secrets, reconciliation, the elect, life, and immortality, to the point that these things become the focus. David caught a glimpse of this and said:

> "When thou sawest a thief, then thou consentedst with him, and hast been made partakers with adulterers." (Ps. 50:18)

The thief can be the thing revealed by the spirit of revelation that will steal you from personal communion with God. One can become so taken with greater and deeper revelations, he continually seeks them, and becomes satisfied with **self**; because of all the wonderful things that are revealed about man, and the part he is to play in God's plan for the ages. Revelation can, and has become a thief. It has stolen praise and worship, prayer and communion with God, gifts and ministries, and even the scriptures. When this happens, one is walking in spiritual adultery, for God is jealous and will share you with no other, not even

---

75 Deuteronomy 6:11-12

the great mysteries about him. We must enter into a rest with God, not with revelations. There is no rest to lay down with revelations. The revelation of rest is to lay down with him.

Many believe themselves to be so mature they can no longer lift their hands and say, "Thank you, Jesus." Jesus has become something of a lower order to them. We may not totally agree on where or what people see about Jesus, but let it be forever settled that the "I AM" Jesus showed us is the only way to the Father. (John 14:6) We need the wisdom of God to bring correction in certain areas. It is our *revelations* that need to be saved, (healed), and filled with the Holy Spirit of all possibilities. It is not the doctrines of religion, nor the revelations of the elect that will save mankind. For example, your beliefs in the rapture, heaven or hell, reconciliation, life, or immortality are not where salvation lies. What you believe about hell or heaven won't save you. Salvation (correction of erroneous thinking) lies in the Holy Spirit's ability through Christ consciousness, which was given to us by Jesus. You who have confessed and received him can find that bond that will unite and bring glory, praise and honor to his name (nature) in you. Until unity is found, it does not matter whose camp you are in, you have not truly found the reality of God. You have only found the things that represent him from different levels. After two thousand years of division and separation due to man's interpretations of God and his Word, don't you think it is past time to find God. After all, only God can straighten this whole thing out.

We have tried to produce new children, yet robbed them of the very experiences that have been used to bring us to our present level of truth. As we return to God and allow his wisdom and direction to lead us into whatever level of ministry is needed, we will see men drawn unto him. This can only happen as he is lifted up, and not the knowledge about him. It is time to turn within us and enter a new communion with our God. We are not to go out and seek these things nor try to make them happen. We need to go behind the veil and minister unto God. (Ez. 44:15-16) Only in that place can we be prepared for a true ministry. Some say this will be done by spirit. But where is spirit and how does spirit express but through yielded vessels: those who are in tune with God to receive instructions and directions. Unenlightened people are not spiritual enough to hear what the spirit has to say. They've got to hear someone's voice, and that is where you come in. They need someone's face to look into and behold the glory of God. They need to behold such a manifestation that they will say, "What manner of man is this?" Then, the moment you get their attention, you will declare: "Don't look at me, look to him that is within." This is how the world will be introduced to the true and living God. Jesus was totally led by the spirit. He knew exactly how to get man to look at him. But the minute they looked at him, he would say; "...the son can do nothing of himself, but what he seeth the Father do...." (John 5:19) He was the expression of the invisible God walking in form. He never attempted on any occasion to turn people to himself, but with every opportunity he spoke of the Father. Even in the words: "When you've seen me, you've seen the Father." (John 14:9) He was reinforcing the destiny of his earthly mission — to always point man to the Father.

There are great surprises in store as we repent (change our minds) of our puffed-up, know-it-all attitudes, and become God's availability to meet man at whatever level he needs to be met. You do not have to leave the place you have come to by knowledge and revelation. Who you are can never be changed. It is because of the awakening you have experienced of who you are, that you are now ready to be God's hand extended to a hurting and seeking world. They may not be ready to hear your wonderful revelations, which were *given to you* so you could become them. As you manifest these revelations, however, what you become will be read and known of all men. (IICor 3:2-3) We have come to a place on our path of progressive truth that God is saying, "***Stop!***" Return unto him and allow direction to come, which will bring understanding and fruit, which will remain. It is not the revelation that all men will be saved that will save all men. It is principles contained in the revelation, that give us the formula of how to bring all men to salvation. This enlightenment will not come by revelation but by God.

Knowledge has revealed that salvation for all men will come through a partnership between God & man. "We are joint heirs with Jesus Christ." (Rom. 8:17) Revelation knowledge has revealed that God is the Savior of all men and will reconcile all things back to Himself. (IICor. 5:18-19) Does that mean all are walking in the reality of salvation? Does it mean the revelation is wrong because we do not see all men coming to God? It simply means the revelation does not have the ability to save one man, much less all men. Many have received a revelation that death can be overcome, as man overcomes disease and walks in divine health, no longer subject to old age and decay. Yet we must again admit, the revelation has had no power to produce life. Does this mean the message of life is wrong? Absolutely not. But again, we can see a divine principle in this. Hearing is only the beginning. It is not the hearing of a revelation that brings life, but the principles contained within the revelation. God holds the only key that will unlock these mechanics. We have heard and seen many wonderful truths, but these are only the pattern, the blueprint. We must now return unto God so he may unlock the reality of these things we've seen by revelation.

There comes the time in the life of a child when he reaches a certain age or maturity and is ready to leave home to begin his own life. It is a very important time and usually the child does not want his parents calling too much or dropping by to check on him. He is grown now and will go through a time of feeling very sufficient within himself. I remember quite well the time I first left home. I made it plain to my parents that I needed my own space and I did not want them hovering over me. Things went well for a while, but I'll never forget the first time that I experienced the trauma of being an adult and on my own. I started thinking about Mom and Dad, and how much I wanted to go home and just sit down and talk to them. I did not want to move back into my old room, as that was all a part of my past. That night I went home; but I went home from where I was. I went back to establish a relationship with my parents from a different level. I wanted to tell them that even though I had a need to be independent and on my own; the fact was, no matter where I went or what I did, they were still my parents. I was still their child and would always need their love. I also needed to know that I could come to them at anytime, and share my joys and heartaches with them knowing they would retain their love for me as their child no matter how old I was. I wanted the freedom to walk back into that relationship from any level that life might take me.

God's sons in the earth have heard a lot of revelation and thought they were grown. We found out God was in us, which made us think we were lords, kings, saviors, etc. For some reason, these great revelations made some believe that any other level of God was childish and immature. Yet in the midst of these wrong interpretations, there is a people returning unto God. They are not returning to their childish ways as they have put away those things. We do not need to go back and pick up our toys, or play the games we use to play; but we are returning to establish a relationship from where we are. We are returning to say, "I know who I am and I am so thankful that I do. I am so glad to know I am of your substance, I am spirit, and in union I am a part of the Christ body. I am so glad I know, by inheritance, I am a son of God, an heir of God and a joint heir with Jesus Christ. I am excited about what I know, but in the midst of all this knowing, I have begun to realize, in spite of the discovery of my deity, **this deity needs a Deity**! This god needs a God! This king needs a King! This lord needs a Lord! This son needs a Son! I am returning to God to establish a relationship with the Most High so I may make him the God above all gods, the King of kings, the Lord of lords." It is time to take our crowns and lay them at his feet. Crowns speak of authority, and there has been an authority given to a people on the earth; but it was given so we might return and give the authority back to him to be expressed in the outer world.

We have been the son who said to his father, "Give me all that belongs to me." Our father richly endowed us with our inheritance through the vehicle of revelation. We have gone out and joined ourselves to a citizen of a far country. After recklessly spending all we had, we found ourselves in the swine pen of human defeat. In the pigpen of human limitations, however, a people are awakening from the hypnotic state of revelation knowledge.[76] There is a people who are coming to their senses and shaking themselves to arise and return to their Father's house. "I will arise, no one is making me; I will arise and choose to make this great return." There has been a pride birthed right along with the birthing of our sonship consciousness. Pride goes before destruction, therefore it must be cleansed from the high places. The son who is now awakening to return to the Father is saying, "I am no more worthy to be called a son, but will be as a servant in my Father's house." True sonship begins when the son understands his own servitude. When sonship is laid down and you are willing to be a servant to all, the Father will give you the ring of authority. He will place his robe of righteousness upon your back, and feed you with meat you know not of.

---

[76] Luke 15:11-32 The story of the Prodigal Son

As we take off our crown[77] of revelation that has filled us with false pride and returned to our Father, there is going to be a celebration of life. Out of death comes life, and out of life comes spirit. Truth is no longer just a shell of revelation. We will continue to grow in the knowledge of the Lord and in divine revelation, but it will no longer be our focus. It will take its proper place.

There was a time when David desired above all else to see the Ark of the Covenant returned home. He called the great men of Israel together, and they bought a new cart to go after the Ark. After retrieving the Ark from the enemy and well into their homeward journey, the oxen stumbled and the Ark began to fall and Uzzah put forth his hand and touched the Ark to keep it from falling. God's anger was kindled against Uzzah, and he died by the Ark. (IISam. 6:7-12) King David was displeased with God and did not understand how such a thing could happen. David's motive was pure and his desire was right to want the Ark to be brought home. The problem was he did not seek the due order of God, but went about it through the reasoning of his own mind. In this we see the place we have arrived today. We've got the revelation of God's plan for the earth, the universe, all mankind and for many generations to come. Now we just need to seek the due order of God to know how to bring it into manifestation. As long as we look to knowledge and to our own strength, we too will cause the death of innocent people. We must seek God for divine guidance to accomplish what we have been shown by revelation.

There is no basic formula or simple answer to know how we are to accomplish this return unto God. This will perhaps be a most intimate, individual dealing. I want to close this chapter on *The Cleansing of the High Place* with a quote from the words of Jeremiah, which reads as follows:

> "Oh Lord you know, remember me and visit me... know that for your sake I suffer and bear reproach. Your words were found and I ate them, and your words were to me a joy and rejoicing of my heart, for I am called by your name...I sat alone because your hand was upon me...Why is my pain perpetual, and my wound incurable, refusing to be healed? Will you indeed be

---

77 *Signifies only head knowledge, not the experience of the heart.*

to me as a deceitful brook, like waters that fail and are uncertain...Therefore, God says: If you return, give up this mistaken tone of distrust and despair, **then** I will give you **again** a settled place of quiet and safety...**If you** separate the precious from the vile, cleansing your own heart from unworthy suspicions concerning God and his faithfulness, you shall be my mouthpiece." (Jer. 15:15-19, Amplified Translation)

I want each of us to hear ourselves in Jeremiah's words,

"Oh God, you know I've lost my church, family, friends and reputation because of the things you've spoken to me, **but** that's all right; I know you understand my suffering and will remember me and visit me. You know the things you have revealed to me have become my very life, and are a joy to me and I want nothing else. You know I am alone and misunderstood because of the revelation that burns within me. I don't mean to complain, it's really all right. I'm proud to be called by your name and not identified with a church or denomination. There is one thing that really bothers me, and I just don't understand. Why does my pain seem to never end? Why do my wounds, sicknesses, heartaches, mental anguish, financial problems, grief and constant fretting about all of these things seem to literally refuse to be healed no matter how much I try? God, surely you have not deceived me into believing I can overcome sickness, old age, mental anguish, worries and death; not that I would ever really think such a thing, but it sure appears that way. I know you have given me a revelation that all of these things can be swallowed up in your life; surely the waters of life you have so freely given will not fail me now."

God's answer to us is as follows: *"Every time you worry and fret over the things I have shown you, you have turned from me. Every time* you allow yourself to be overtaken with thoughts of the external affairs of life, it causes you to doubt me. This song you sing of "Woe is me, and how long Lord?" is to me a tone that cries out from your heart as distrust and despair. In spite of all I have spoken to you, your heart continues to be filled with unworthy suspicions about my faithfulness. You never doubt me when you are caught up into the heavens. It is only when you begin to focus on the physical, external things that you become afraid. How long will you continue to look for the living among the dead? I do not dwell in the mirage of memories of past defeats nor of hopes for tomorrow. I long for you to return unto me. I long to take the many revelations I have given you and show you the formula for life hidden within each principle. Come unto me, for I understand that you are weary and heavy laden. Return to me, and learn to trust me with all your heart; look no longer to revelations for salvation and deliverance. Let me cause you to walk in my faith, and know that I am able to cause my word to accomplish the purpose for which it was given. You must come to me as a child, and again learn to lean upon me, for in this place I can give you wisdom and guidance to cleanse your heart of the many unworthy suspicions you yet hold of me. The marks of death that cause doubt and fear must be erased. I desire to be your Father and to lead you gently back to a place of peace and safety. I have placed you into the realms of humanity so you might experience all that creation has need to be delivered of, but know that the day of these experiences can soon be fulfilled in your lives. Learn my compassion and learn my mercy, and in so doing you shall free yourself from the chains of human bondage. Of your own freewill, come and lay all that I have given you at my feet, and together we can build a habitation wherein all can dwell."

From Knowledge To Expression

Our journey through revelation knowledge can be the greatest part of our walk through the realms of humanity, *if* we use what we have been given as tools to bring life. We have been as a doctor or lawyer who has spent many years preparing to take his place in the world. Now he is using the principles he has learned to help others.

Many of us have come to a place of maturity. We have awakened to the fact it is not what you know that matters, but how you use what you know. I cannot emphasize, too often, how important it is to take the knowledge we have been given, and allow spirit to teach us the mechanics that will produce it into our outer worlds. We must stop expecting a rapture (escape). And we must also stop the mental gymnastics of ***mind over matter***, and realize we need God.

> "Truly in vain is salvation hoped for from the hills, and from the multitude of mountains: truly in the Lord our God is the salvation of Israel. For shame hath devoured the labor of our Fathers from our youth...we lie down in our shame and our confusion covereth us: for we have sinned[78] against the Lord our God...and have not obeyed the voice of the Lord our God. (Jer. 3:23-25)

Hills and mountains speak of great revelations that have been given in the high place from God. On this pathway of revelation, faith in God has been replaced by faith in revelation. When man taps into his God substance and begins to focus on who he is, God is often no longer considered to be a part of what he now needs. This has caused a condition to appear in the high places that retains shame and confusion, and has caused a sin against God. I am aware these words are foreign to many. It is for this reason that God has drawn me aside and begun to drop these things into my heart, and I feel a great responsibility to shepherd the revelations I have given the people.

The line between truth and error is truly a ***fine*** one and we have come to the place in our journey that we can no longer throw out these ***weighty*** words without using wisdom and understanding. But regardless of the words being spoken by us who have been given this great knowledge, confusion and shame continues to plague us, for it appears no fruit is being produced. This can be corrected, however, as we begin our return back to God. Remember that sin means simply

---

78 The word sin comes from the Greek word "hamartano" meaning to miss the mark (nature).

missing the mark. When knowledge is compared to our everyday reality, we have surely missed the mark.

The hell man is still walking through is created by his own unbelief in the God of his salvation; not the god he is, or the god of his great revelations, but the very God of the Universe. The *I Am* stepped out of eternity and took upon himself the form of humanity to show man his deity, his God substance. This was not done so man might become a god unto himself; but through this realization of his God-substance, he could find a place of communion with the great I Am. By doing this, God could become all in man's life bringing forth a full manifestation at all levels. Jesus became our door from earth to heaven, and he is the only entrance from the material world into the spiritual world. He is also a door from the spiritual into the physical world. There must be a people walking in the earth realm who are now willing to become Jesus' door from the heavens back into the earth. He is searching for that availability and that access so his will can be done in the earth realm as it is in the heavens. This is the reason you have been shown your God likeness, not for you, but for him. It is only through this awakening that he can come to the earth to bring salvation, healing and deliverance to the conditions that have been created by the mind of man.

I hear the words of God speaking to a people in the earth saying, "Call upon Me in the day of trouble; I will deliver thee and thou shalt glorify Me" (Ps. 50:15)

When one begins to walk in the realm of an open heaven and tap into the stream of the unveiling of the mysteries and secrets of God, the mind can bring the deception that you are calling on God. When in reality, you are attempting to find answers by searching through principles the mind has learned. The mind can bring condemnation, and you may ask yourself the following questions: "Why do you need help? You know better than to feel and act like this. What is wrong with you?" If this is the case, you might ask, "What is the revelation for?" You must have knowledge, for without it you will perish. The key is to take your knowledge back to God and allow him to give you wisdom and understanding to unlock what is contained within the things you have seen. We are not to glorify revelation, but we are to glorify God. If revelation had been allowed to totally work in our lives at this point, we would never find the true God. Revelation is given to establish and set divine order, but it cannot bring healing, deliverance, salvation, or help in time of trouble. Only God can do this. The only substance of revelation is God.

It is time to return to our first love. Revelation cannot continue to be our greatest love. Ideas are formed from knowledge, and without realizing it, the idea itself becomes your god. The things you begin to believe about God forms images in your mind, and you bow down to the image thinking it is God. God is a jealous God, and he will not share you with another; not even the ideas that have been formed by the things he has revealed. These revelations are essential, but they were only given to bring you up to the level in which God dwells, so that he might manifest himself to you at that level. Revelation will never give us peace, joy or immortality; it will never cause us to overcome sickness, disease, old age or death. Aren't you tired of being caught into a mental heaven while your body remains in the torment of hell?

As I awoke early one morning, it was as if I overheard a conversation between my spirit and my body. Spirit said, "I have gone to prepare a place for you that where I am you may be also." The body is not to be left in hell. The spirit is beginning to send forth a call to the external world to **arise**. It is wonderful and exciting to go into our mental heavens, and to know that **within** all is well, yet for all this knowing, it brings no change on the outside. As the mind goes up, it brings the body down through the fire.

In the first half of our journey we have taken all the natural and spiritualized it. We took the natural heaven, the natural hell, the physical Jesus, the literal return, etc., and spiritualized all of them. Everything in the natural realm has been looked upon as spiritual. As we make the curve, beginning our return and ascension back to God, just as the natural was spiritualized, we will now see the spiritual become naturalized. What we have looked for in the natural realm has only been the spiritual; but now the spiritual is going to be naturalized, or materialized into our external world. Life, health, peace, joy and prosperity will no longer only be a spiritual revelation, but will become materialized in your external world as the word is made flesh.

God desires that our lives be full and complete. Revelation has given us the knowledge to know this is possible. But it is not just enough to know and believe; it is time for it to become a way that can be touched and handled. As the redeemed of the Lord return unto God, they shall obtain the reality of the great revelation knowledge that has only been on their head. We shall begin to see sorrow flee out of our external world. What took place in one man two thousand years ago (an incarnation) can happen to a corporate man as spirit is incarnated into the flesh of a many membered body. We must, as Job did, wait until our change comes. This change will happen when spirit enters our bodies and raises the vibratory frequency to the level of Spirit. This is the coming of the Christ in physical form.

> "In returning and rest ye shall be saved, quietness and confidence shall be your strength." (Is. 30:15)

It is as we return to God to establish a new communion with him that we will be able to enter into a rest that will bring quietness to the mind and strength to the body. As long as you look at revelations one minute, and the manifestation of your external affairs of life the next, you will find no rest. Revelations can't save you; knowledge can't save you; mind believing can't save you. But God, who waits patiently for us to return to him, holds the key that will unlock the principles contained within all we have learned. We will then see the body integrated with soul and spirit to make us whole. "Wilt thou be made whole?" (John 5:6)

> "Be not deceived, God is not mocked..." (Gal. 6:7)

This scripture tells us man is not to deceive himself. You are the only one that can cause deception within your own mind. A mind filled with revelation can be deceived without the wisdom of God to build a new consciousness. Revelation has not been given so we can act it out with our own faculties, energy or strength. Revelation must be brought into alignment with spirit in order for God to be the one who lives his life through you; not you attempting to live your life by the knowledge you have received. Revelation can puff a person up by causing him to begin acting like he has something, when all he actually has is a revelation. That is deception. God does not want you to act out the things you have heard. That is mocking God. It is time to stop acting out our righteousness, sanctification, victory, joy, peace or anything else. As long as you are acting the part, you are not allowing God to bring the reality of His own manifestation.

How can we enter into rest and stop mocking God as long as we are trying to act out the things we have heard? We must first understand our union with Christ.

> "But he that is joined to the Lord is one spirit."(I Cor. 6:17)

This is the union that will break the separation of you and God, and make of the two — one new man. Let's not confuse the facts, however, by expecting an awakening to this union to bring instant change externally. That frame of mind is what has caused us to turn from God and begin to look to revelation. You must still accept the individual you are outwardly, but inwardly understand your union or oneness with Christ. It is time to realize it is this inner union that will produce whatever change may be needed externally. Awakening, recognition and progression are to bring the understanding it is he living *his* life through us, *not* us living *our* life for him. Please hear these words, because you can only allow this to happen as you return to God and not to the revelation spoken in these words.

I want to take the liberty to paraphrase, as spirit spoke it to me, from (Gal. 2:20):

> "The independent I has been permanently crucified, nevertheless I live, yet not I as a separate being, but the spirit of Christ living in union with my spirit, and the life which the unified I lives in the flesh, it lives by his faith uniquely expressing *himself* through my container."

The idea that I am separate from him must be crucified. This crucifixion happens through awakening and the recognition of our union with God. The unified I lives his life by the faith of God; not his own faith. There is a difference in the faith *of* God and faith *in* God. Faith *in* is your faith (belief), which wavers and is limited, and is controlled by external circumstances. The faith ***of***[79] God is never limited, never wavers, and is never effected by external conditions. Until the life you live in the flesh is lived by God's faith and not your own faith, you will never know true righteousness. (Rom. 3:22) Revelation has brought our faith into a higher level than when we walked under the bondage of religion. We must realize that most people are acting out, in other words, mocking a new way of life formed in their consciousness by the things they have caught a glimpse of by the spirit. Revelation brings the awakening, but, many times, out of that awakening the mind steps in, takes the revelation and begins to act it out. This is why it must all be taken back to God so he can bring true inner recognition as we wait upon him.

All revelation truth that has been spoken in this day must find an embodiment to walk the earth. This truth has moved us from one realm or consciousness to another, but each time it has happened we have simply moved over and not up. Revelation does not bring ascension, as all knowledge is on the same level. One may have a revelation of salvation by grace and a confession of the Lord Jesus, at one end, and a revelation of the reconciliation of all men at the other end. Yet each end is only a portion of truth, unable to contain all there is of God; neither can revelation bring the manifestation of the things revealed. You can receive one revelation after the other and only be moving over and not up. Moving over is progression, but it is not the ultimate intention. How can we know if we have begun to move up and not just over through the vehicle of revelation? The answer is when no person, place or thing controls your feelings, moods or emotions. "If we can meet with ***both*** triumph and disaster, and treat these two impostors as the same, ours is the world and everything that's in it." (Kipling) Both triumph and disaster are called impostors because they represent the duality of good and evil. As long as we know good and evil at any level, we will continue to be controlled by feelings, moods, and emotions. To see both triumph and disaster alike is going beyond all duality. There is a place beyond knowledge where God and man can meet. It has taken knowledge to move you to this place, but it will now take God to produce the truth contained within knowledge.

---

79 The word "of" in the Greek means "out from".

> "That you may really come to know practically through experience for yourselves the love of Christ which far surpasses mere knowledge without experience. That you may be filled through all your being unto all the fullness of God, that it may have the richest measure of the divine presence and become a body wholly filled and flooded with God himself. Now unto him Who, by (in consequence of) the action of his power that is at work within us, is able to carry out his purpose and do superabundantly, far over and above all that we dare ask, or think - infinitely above our highest prayers, desires, thoughts, hopes or dreams;. To him be the glory…" (Eph. 3:19-21 Amplified)

This is not hearing a revelation or accepting a doctrine, but it is intimately experiencing the love of God. This is not speaking of something that is **about** God. It is God himself standing in the congregation of the mighty, judging among those who have awakened to their God likeness: those who have walked in fellowship and communion with him. Can you understand it has been necessary for us to walk the way of revelation knowledge? This walk has brought us to a place of returning unto God so he can overshadow the word that has been revealed and bring it into expression. You cannot overshadow yourself. It does not matter what you know or believe; it will take God to produce the manifestation in the flesh. Revelation knowledge has created some powerful thoughts, dreams and hopes; but God will bypass them all and do super abundantly above all we have created in our quest for knowledge. Knowledge holds man in delusion until it is returned unto God.

We have taken revelation knowledge and done all we could to change our external worlds, but it has been to no avail. As we return to God, reactions will change for we will be tuned to a higher vibration of thinking and living. Knowledge has not brought the reality of an overcoming life, because we have continued to judge by the same standard of good and evil. Overcoming is not changing things. We have taken knowledge and struggled to change people, places and situations; but it has not worked. Overcoming is a change in the way one thinks and sees the world around him. You cannot make this happen, for it is only as God becomes our focus and is given the availability to live in and through us will we see the world come to a conscious knowing of their salvation. As God stands in a body of people, he will use our minds, imaginations and creative faculties to draw all men unto him, not unto us. The spirit in union with imagination becomes a creative force. To see all men awakened, we must hold that vision within and treat every man alike, and through that availability freedom comes. Creative love, which is the strongest force in the Universe, holds the mind in pureness and births an expression into the outer world.

As we make the curve and begin our return and ascension back to God, a new song will fill the land. You will not learn this song from a book, for it is a song above all language, it is the very vibration of the universe; and it will neutralize the destructive forces that fill our land. We are his creators as we stand in union with the Creator, allowing him to create through us. Turn your focus back to God, no longer focusing on your revelation knowledge. Stop trying to declare truth and allow God to declare all that he is. A new beginning is dawning within the consciousness of those who return unto God. It is a breaking forth of spiritual awareness to awaken us from sleep. Heaven and earth are about to kiss; knowledge and truth are about to meet; God and man are coming face to face. The Day Star is rising in our hearts as we return to the place in God we came out of. In this returning we shall present God a physical habitation, enabling him to fulfill his ultimate intention, which is not just to save all men: it is to fill all things, in heaven, in earth, and throughout the universe with himself. Do not throw the knowledge you have received away, but gather it all together, and take it, and lay it at his feet. Out of this shall a new appearing break forth in your earth as God stands in his temple in full communion — as the union of God and man becomes a living expression.

David Hulse, D.D.

Back Into The Upper Room

The theme of returning can be summed up in the word - paradox. Webster defines the word paradox as "a statement that is seemingly contradictory or opposed to common sense and yet is perhaps true, a tenet contrary to received opinions, something with seeming contradictory qualities or phases." In other words, it expresses an appearance of something that seems to be going one direction, yet is actually going another. We see a perfect example of a paradox in the life of Jesus. He told the disciples it was expedient that he go away at the young age of thirty-three and a half years. They did not understand, because of their great love for him in the physical realm, they would have held him in an earthly limitation. Jesus knew he was limited if he stayed with them as only a man. He knew that he had to go away to get closer. He went away to be made spirit, so that when he returned he would be in them, and not just with them. This is what is taking place today. It may appear something is being taken away, but in reality it is about to come closer.

As we return to God, we are going to experience a full re-evaluation of every word that has been given to the Church for the past two thousand years. We are going to see subjects such as salvation, Holy Spirit baptism, praise and worship take on a new meaning and birth a new experience and new expression in our lives. The paradox is, it would appear we are going back to the experiences of the orders of religion that we have been called out of, yet we are not going back but going forward as we return to God. This statement, seemingly contradictory, and going totally against opinions we have acquired through the knowledge of the past few years, is actually a true statement. When we met God in the experience of our awakening, being filled with the baptism of the Holy Spirit, it was tremendous. In the moment of our awakening, we began to discover God for the first time in the earth realm. But soon after the moment of our experience of an inner awakening, religion stepped in and began to teach us their doctrines and traditions concerning salvation and the Holy Spirit. I submit to you today, as wonderful as our walk thus far may have been, we have never known the fullness of salvation or been filled with the fullness of the Holy Spirit. God has things to say to us concerning these subjects that will totally revolutionize our lives.

Recently, there was a young lady in a meeting who expressed a desire to be filled with the Holy Spirit. Throughout the meeting my heart was drawn to her, and every time I would start to go and pray for her, the Lord would stop me. Some of the people tried to pray her through[80]. Needless to say, nothing did any good. My heart was filled with compassion as I felt the sincerity of her heart, yet I knew I did not have the answers to what her heart was crying out for. I could not present the Holy Spirit to her from the level I have known it. Out of this, God began to appear and present us with a glimpse of a dimension of a Holy Spirit experience that I want to share with you. Let's start with this quote from Hannah Hunard's book, *Steps to the Kingdom*. This is Peter's point of view, according to the author, as to what took place on the day of Pentecost:

> "Now I will tell you more of what happened on the day of Pentecost. We were gathered together praying and studying the things our Master had taught us, reconsidering them in the light of what he had revealed to us through his death, resurrection and the teaching he had given us during the forty days before he ascended into the heavenly realm. Everything took on a completely new significance in our understanding and suddenly we heard a sound from heaven. He paused and said, 'How can I describe the sound? It was a heavenly sound that none of us could ever forget.' Luke tells you in Acts that the Holy Spirit was as a mighty rushing wind, as though the breath of God was blowing out of the unseen world into their hearts. The word Luke uses means a ringing sound like a bell or a great rush of wind striking a mighty harp, for we ourselves were the harp. When the rushing wind came each of us vibrated to the touch like individual notes from a musical instrument. The wind struck a chord in each of us that gave forth its own note and sound in response. It spoke the name that God had

---

80   *An old Pentecostal phrase meaning to pray one through one's disbelief to a place of receptivity.*

breathed into each of us when he brought us forth out of the dust as individual creatures. The lost forgotten name we recognized as our own. At that moment we knew the meaning and purpose for which we had been created, our own special place in the whole marvelous scheme of things. The sound woke this responsive chord in each heart, quickened to life and a burning desire to fulfill the special purpose of God for us. It touched chords that as they responded burst forth into a glorious harmony. How long we remained there in that room responding to this breath of God and giving forth this heavenly harmony, I do not know. Our tongues uttered notes and tones of a great musical symphony. It was the sound of this that caused people to gather in the street outside, awe-struck and spell-bound. We were not preaching, we were simply responding to him in tones like musical notes in heavenly harmonics, expressing the desires and longings that had been awakened in our hearts. But, the tones that they heard awakened in the people outside longings and aspirations like those we ourselves were experiencing. They heard in that sound something that spoke to their own hearts as plainly as though they were being spoken to in their own Mother tongue. Each one heard the spirit speaking the name of his or her own ideal nature buried away and lost under years of forgetfulness. It was not until the Holy Wind in the upper room ceased blowing that we were aware of the crowds outside. Peter went down to speak to them and he heard them saying, 'Look, how is it that we hear each in our own language in which we were born? We hear them speaking in our tongues the wonderful works of God.' Matthew paused and said, 'It was never again quite like that, never again with great crowds gathering in public streets.' But, over and over again when groups of believers and inquirers were listening to the preaching the wind blew again. The breath reached the chords of all our hearts and brought forth the same response of awakening desire, stirring us to Christ-consciousness. It was the language of love, a Universal language, just as music is universal evoking wordless response from the depths of one's being. From that time, from the moment our minds were opened, or baptized into full consciousness of Christ, there was a new note and a new tone in the voice of every one of us, especially when we were preaching. It was the tone of burning love, the love of Christ within us. Then without effort, we discovered that the tone of the new indwelling love had extraordinary power to affect others. Whenever we spoke we were able to ring a bell in our hearts to name their own secret names and summon their inner natures to answer the call."

Let's consider the possibility of a new Pentecost; reconsidering it in the light of what God has revealed to us by revelation knowledge. Is it possible, as we return to God, everything we have known up to this point could take on a completely new significance in our understanding? Can we dare to take another look at the true baptism of the Holy Spirit and true praise and worship? This must be taken out of the mental realm. Otherwise, when we sing a song, say hallelujah, glory, or praise his name, they are empty sounds and carry no spirit in them. They are empty shells of mental sounds: notes with no melody. Until the spirit puts the sounds together, there is no melody; and it is the melody that goes forth and touches lives and hearts. Empty shells of notes void of spirit give forth an uncertain sound. When the vibration of spirit crosses the strings of our heart, the combination of sounds will bring forth the song out of Zion that will awaken your inner Christ nature. In the process, others will be touched in the awakening. Can you hear it? Whatever happened to the one hundred and twenty on the day of Pentecost also happened to those on the outside; three thousand were touched in their spirit; they came and began to ask what was going on. No man can achieve for themselves alone. There is not one thing God can give you that is for you only, but everything you are given is going to send forth a vibration into the Universe touching thousands of people. It's an inner thing, that's why Christ is doing an inner work. It is not in the outer, but it's in the collective consciousness of man that we are connected. This is why there are areas of your psyche that you do not understand and feel you have no control of. Your circumstances are not unique. You can analyze your life all you want to, but there are areas in your life that have been passed on to you from past generations. As you understand this and allow the spirit to enter that part of you, what is loosed in earth will be loosed in heaven. This vibration will literally shake heaven and be a part of the creation of new heavens.

We have come to a time, while waiting upon spirit to birth a new appearing, the outer sounds of praise and worship will be the effects of an inner response. The Holy Spirit experience is the awakening and recognition of the name you were given before coming into the earth realm: the one you have forgotten. It's what God called you before the foundation of the world. It is a name you once knew before learning earthly language. As this name is heard, it will awaken a nature that lies asleep deep within. As we are awakened, we will sing, "I once was blind, but now I see. I once was lost, but now I'm found." It sings *Amazing Grace* out of an awakening, not out of a hymnbook. That's what the Holy Spirit does. It's not some emotional experience of chills running down your spine. It is an enhancement from this human knowing of yourself to a God knowing of who you were and have been all along and will always be — a name that knows no past or future, but is. It is the

Conclusion

We stand at a most awesome and wonderful time. It is a time of awakening to the forgotten essence of who we are, where we came from, and why we are on this earth. Be aware of your importance as a critical part of God's creative plan for both the earth and the universe. The things you choose today, tomorrow or next week are far greater than you have dared to believe. You are at a place of new and wonderful beginnings, which will have great effect on the future of the world. Become aware of your responsibility, so your release is no longer held in captivity. You are the means by which God will love all of his creation. Release the past and the future and learn to live each day: each moment in the presence of God. Live in his presence so you are no longer restricted and limited to the pain and heartache of human conditions. There is a way to transcend all realms that are void of life. But it is of vital importance to know that each realm of darkness can only be transcended as you walk through it and become the light to dispel the darkness. If you fear or dread, you can be momentarily consumed in the illusions, which have so effectively made their mark upon this world. There are steps of preparation that must be taken. Only when each, in his private and individual walk with God, begins to prepare to see the release of all that God has purposed, will we see life begin to pick up momentum. Make up your mind today to become the expression of God to those who surround your life. Soon it will begin to have dramatic effect upon all who feel the touch of your substance.

I trust you will not take the words written in this book lightly, but pray & meditate over them, and ask the Father to expand and release greater understanding as you open yourself to the wonderful potential that lies in embracing all truth. Don't allow yourself to be fenced in by names and labels. Dare to step outside of every limitation that is daring to hold you from knowing the reality of God. People are searching for someone who can love and understand them with no strings attached. Dare to be a lover, rather that a fighter, and you will see your world literally transform before your very eyes.

LWM Message-of-the-Month

The Message-of-the-month (M.O.M.) is designed to keep you informed of the message flowing through David each month. The LWM Staff picks a 60-minute CD each month that best represents the message of David. This CD is then sent to all who choose to participate in the M.O.M. program. The M.O.M. also contains current announcements of upcoming events and excerpts from upcoming guest speakers. It is an excellent vehicle for you to stay current with David's message between the times that he visits your area.

As a participant, we ask for a minimum monthly donation of $15.00. Many people donate more than 15.00 each month. These funds make up nearly 1/4 of the LWM monthly budget. This program also allows David to travel to new areas of the country in which he plant seeds of hope to new groups. Many times, in the beginning, these groups cannot yet support a weekend with David on their own. Through the M.O.M. David can travel as he is led, allowing these groups to grow.

We encourage you to share the M.O.M. with others as an introduction to LWM. As we raise our individual consciousness, we have a responsibility to extend the vehicles that assisted us to others. The M.O.M. serves as an excellent vehicle for reaching out to others who are searching.

To sign up for the M.O.M. call 937-912-9229 or visit us at www. lightwithin.com. We have several vehicles for you to make this donation including Automatic Bank Draft, placing the donation on your credit card or sending in the donation each month in the envelope included in each M.O.M.

We encourage you to become a co-creator with LWM through participating in the Message-of-the-month.

Get the Latest Information...
Do you want to stay on top of what is coming through David each month? We invite you to join the Message-of-the-Month. *For a monthly donation of $15 or more, you get:*
- √ The best of David each month on CD
- √ Personal message from David
- √ Special offers to M.O.M. Participants
- √ The latest schedule information
- √ Announcements on upcoming events

Call 937-912-9229 or email somaenergetics@lightwithin.com to join today!

About The Author... David Hulse, D.D.

Awakening the Body of Christ

Throughout his years of spiritual searching, David has challenged many traditional doctrines, theologies and dogmas. He has inspired numerous individuals toward a journey of self-discovery by sharing his own journey.

After receiving the baptism of the Holy Spirit at 16 years old, David was challenged to look again at many of the beliefs taught to him during his fundamental literalist upbringing. David was shown by the Holy Spirit that God's pure word was locked up **in** (inside) the parables for a generation to come who would not walk as their forefathers [Psalms 78], but who would speak these mysteries plainly of the Father. [John 16:25] Confronting the challenge of his childhood beliefs, David wrestled with the emptiness and loss, leaving him angry and anxious about his future ministry.

As David has traveled through various beliefs about God, Hell, Resurrection, Sin, Satan, Earth-bound Spirits and Law & Grace, he now sees himself as a bridge between the old and the new. Each has a contribution to make to the enrichment of the other. These booklets, which make up this book, were written during his transition. Since very little transitional material is available for those searching, this book as been released to fill that void.

Today David is dedicated to assisting the body of Christ to grow up in every way and into all things… to full maturity, building itself up in love. [Ephesians 4:15-16] His stirring presentations of intuitive wisdom will inspire and challenge you to move from believing in God to the experiential realm of knowing God and your co-creative role toward manifestation of the kingdom of God on earth as it is in heaven.

....

A companion study guide is available FREE at www.lightwithin.com/look_book.htm

This guide can also be used for small study groups.

For More Information: www.lightwithin.com or email david@lightwithin.com